Cambridge Elements

Elements in Religion and Monotheism
edited by
Paul K. Moser
Loyola University Chicago
Chad Meister
*Affiliate Scholar, Ansari Institute for Global Engagement with Religion,
University of Notre Dame*

THE POLITICS
OF MONOTHEISM

Ragnar M. Bergem
*MF Norwegian School of Theology, Religion
and Society*

CAMBRIDGE
UNIVERSITY PRESS

Shaftesbury Road, Cambridge CB2 8EA, United Kingdom

One Liberty Plaza, 20th Floor, New York, NY 10006, USA

477 Williamstown Road, Port Melbourne, VIC 3207, Australia

314–321, 3rd Floor, Plot 3, Splendor Forum, Jasola District Centre, New Delhi – 110025, India

103 Penang Road, #05–06/07, Visioncrest Commercial, Singapore 238467

Cambridge University Press is part of Cambridge University Press & Assessment, a department of the University of Cambridge.

We share the University's mission to contribute to society through the pursuit of education, learning and research at the highest international levels of excellence.

www.cambridge.org
Information on this title: www.cambridge.org/9781009509749

DOI: 10.1017/9781009349260

© Ragnar M. Bergem 2024

First published 2024

A catalogue record for this publication is available from the British Library

ISBN 978-1-009-50974-9 Hardback
ISBN 978-1-009-34928-4 Paperback
ISSN 2631-3014 (online)
ISSN 2631-3006 (print)

The Politics of Monotheism

Elements in Religion and Monotheism

DOI: 10.1017/9781009349260
First published online: December 2024

Ragnar M. Bergem
MF Norwegian School of Theology, Religion and Society

Author for correspondence: Ragnar M. Bergem, Ragnar.m.bergem@mf.no

Abstract: Monotheism, the belief in the One True God, seems to have an ambiguous role in political life: On the one hand, monotheism may foster the inclusion of everybody, regardless of identity or background. On the other, monotheistic religions demand submission to a singular revealed truth, distinguish between faithful and the heretics, and thus seemingly promote an antagonistic and tribalistic politics. What, then, are the political implications of the monotheistic belief in absolute truth? This Element traces the Enlightenment origins of our contemporary debates about monotheism and argues that these debates reflect a deeper Western ambivalence towards religion. It does so while discussing both secular and Christian critics of the politics of monotheism. The Element contends that there is no singular politics of monotheism, and that we can only approach monotheism's political significance if we take seriously the various ways in which truth is represented in political life in monotheistic traditions.

Keywords: monotheism, politics of truth, representation, idolatry, political theology

ISBNs: 9781009509749 (HB), 9781009349284 (PB), 9781009349260 (OC)
ISSNs: 2631-3014 (online), 2631-3006 (print)

Contents

1 Introduction

In 1999, the Salafi jihadist terrorist group 'Jama'at al-Tawhid wal-Jihad' was founded in Jordan. The name literally means 'Group of Monotheism and Jihad'. In 2004, the group pledged allegiance to al-Qaeda. After a series of changes in leadership and titles, in 2013, the then-leader Abu Bakr al-Baghdadi changed the group into the Islamic State of Iraq and the Levant. In an early variety of the Islamic State's creed, the first article declares the 'necessity of destroying and eradicating all manifestations of idolatry (*shirk*) and [the necessity of] prohibiting those things that lead to it' (Bunzel 2015, 38). As Mark Juergensmeyer notes, ISIS thought of itself as part of an apocalyptic struggle, a cosmic war between 'religion and antireligion'.[1]

The invasions, conflicts, and revolutions in the Middle East occupied the public spotlight during the first two decades of the new millennium. Western military aggression, the war on terrorism, and widespread political unrest fuelled ardent debate about the role of religion in Western countries. There was a fear that Samuel Huntington's thesis about the 'Clash of Civilizations' had, after all, something to it (Huntington 1996; Haynes 2021). In public discourse and academic debate, commentators and intellectuals fiercely discussed what role monotheism played in political conflicts. Were we not seeing a clash of monotheisms expressed in the Christian imperialism of the United States and the Islamism of terrorist groups or states? While some critics identified religion itself as a problem, others thought monotheism in particular was the culprit. Jean-Luc Nancy, the French philosopher, wrote about 'the war of monotheism' and claimed that the war in Iraq was a sign that a civilisation based on monotheism was coming up to its limit. The West could only survive if it invented 'a new way of relating to "value", to the "absolute", to "truth"' (Nancy 2003, 53).

Despite the fall of ISIS and the Western withdrawal from Afghanistan and Iraq, the question of the politics of monotheism and its potential for conflict has not disappeared from the scene in recent years. After Russia's occupation of Crimea in 2014 and the full-scale invasion of Ukraine in 2022, the focus had abruptly shifted from the Arab world to Russia – at a time when the attention of Western countries was gradually turning towards Southeast Asia. Once again, war reflects religious division: within the Orthodox Church and between Russia and the West (Hovorun 2022; Benedikter 2023). Kirill, the Patriarch of Moscow, has strongly supported the Putin regime and portrayed the conflict with the West as a fight against the anti-Christ.

---

[1] Juergensmeyer (2017, 193) also notes that this dualism would seem to run counter to the strict notion of unity in Islam, but that this demand for unity may precisely lead to a comic struggle against dualisms, not least the secularistic division between the religious and the sacred.

The 'turn to religion' in the decades around the millennium led to wide-ranging research on the relationship between religion and violence (Juergensmeyer, Kitts, and Jerryson 2013). If we want to understand the sociopolitical potential of monotheistic religion, however, we cannot focus on the question of violence alone, lest we risk reducing monotheism to something extraneous to normal, functioning political institutions. Even if monotheism's potential for conflict remains a key question in contemporary debates, it does at least deserve to be phrased as a broader political question. What, exactly, is the politics of monotheism? How does the belief in one God motivate political action, how does it shape conceptions of political life, and what is its potential for promoting peace or conflict? Although these questions were hardly new, they were fiercely debated in the decades around the turn of the millennium.

This Element is not the place to discuss every, or even most of the important, questions related to the politics of monotheism. Instead, it will approach this broad field by focusing on one aspect: that of truth. It will, put simply, assess the validity of Nancy's claim that the issue of the politics of monotheism is to do with how we relate to the absolute and the truth. The major religious traditions most usually described as monotheistic – Judaism, Islam, and Christianity – all confess the belief in one God, who is the truth, and they deem it of supreme importance to get the right relationship to that truth. This conviction that human life is ultimately determined by its relationship to the One True God is a source of great worry for some critics. While the confession in one God, who is the truth, may ground a sense of communion among all people and nations, it can also divide people, draw a line, and intensify antagonisms. And it is precisely the antagonistic potential of the adherence to absolute truth that has so many people with liberal and democratic sensibilities worried.

Thus, one notable scholar of religion, Jan Assmann, has claimed that monotheism is characterised by the 'Mosaic distinction': the absolute distinction between true and false religion, implied by the Mosaic law, and especially the first commandment, which, among other things, says that 'you shall have no other God before me' (Exodus 20:2).[2] It is this distinction between true worship and idolatry when actualised in political life and mobilised by mission-oriented religions (Christianity and Islam) that proves so divisive and dangerous, Assmann believes. While Judaism employs the Mosaic distinction to guard the boundaries of God's chosen people and thus 'exclude itself' from the rest of the world, Christianity and Islam seek to expand God's people to everybody and impose the dualism between true and false religion onto the world. From this

---

[2] Biblical citations are from the New Revised Standard Version. I follow the Augustinian table, common in Catholicism and many forms of Protestantism, in including both the demand for exclusivity and the prohibition against graven images as part of the first commandment.

perspective, ISIS' violent state-building in Syria and Iraq, the persecution of the Cathars in the Middle Ages, or the early modern Spanish 'extirpation' of Andean religion are just some instances of the Mosaic distinction at work (Mills 1997).

Secularists or people of no religion are not alone in articulating such concerns. Religious thinkers, including those in the Christian tradition, have worried about the dangers of monotheism. In the early twentieth century, the German Church historian Erik Peterson (1890–1960) pointed to how Christian monotheism was mobilised in the early Church to legitimate the newly Christianised Roman Empire. He claimed that only a developed conception of God as a Trinity could end a 'political theology' based on monotheism. Peterson's argument influenced theologians writing in the second half of the century, including Leonardo Boff and Jürgen Moltmann. A more recent critique – from quite a different theological stance – has come from the American theologian Laurel C. Schneider. She claims that the 'contemporary clash of exclusivist monotheisms – Christian, Muslim, and Jewish – or rather the clash of nations and movements deeply shaped by monotheistic claims, sharply illustrate the very current proximity (and vulnerability) of the monotheistic sublime idea to ideological battles for ideological and economic supremacy and for political legitimacy and control' (Schneider 2008, 25–26). Schneider maintains that 'Christian monotheism is empire theology', propagating a 'totalitarian' logic of 'the One' (Schneider 2008, 4–5).

But what is monotheism? The notion is deceptively simple but surprisingly hard to define. According to its plainest definition, monotheism refers to the belief in one God – 'Eingottglaube' according to the *Handbuch religionswissenschaftlicher Grundbegriffe* (Lang 1988, 148). The classic examples of such a belief are to be found in the religious traditions of Judaism, Christianity, and Islam. A paradigmatic proclamation of monotheism is the *Shema Yisrael* 'Hear, O Israel: The Lord is our God, the Lord alone' (Deuteronomy 6:4). This is a proclamation that Christians also affirm. Similarly, the first of the Five Pillars of Islam, the *Shahada* ('the testimony'), states: 'There is no god but Allah, and Muhammad is his messenger.' The Shahada expresses the absolute oneness (*Tawhid*) of God, the very heart of Islamic theology (Ibrahim 2022).

And yet, as soon as one moves past the deceptive simplicity of a numerical delimitation, monotheism fragments into a multitude of religious traditions and philosophical perspectives. The *Handbuch* distinguishes *prophetic* monotheism, which is exclusivist, from *philosophical* monotheism, which may tolerate a polytheistic pantheon (Lang 1988, 150). Then there is the notion of *henotheism*, which is a temporary exaltation of one god among many, or *monolatry*, which is a permanent worship of one god, without denying the existence of others.

Monotheism can be associated with various beliefs that we sometimes take to be opposite. It can be monistic yet also dualistic or pluralistic. It may declare the sovereignty of God, even while it admits an adversary or a whole swathe of other deities. 'Polytheistic' religions – Hinduism, for example – can be described as monotheistic at heart since there is no inherent contradiction between the belief in a pantheon of gods and a transcendent deity beyond every subordinate divinity (Flood 2020). And then there is the issue that monotheism has, at times in history, been described as a kind of atheism (Buckley 1990, 1–13). To complicate the matter further, internal and external critics have denied that Christianity, the largest monotheistic religion, is, in fact, monotheistic. Depending on one's definition, one can find monotheism not only in Judaism, Islam, or Christianity but also in Zoroastrianism, Akhenatenism in ancient Egypt, or in Sikhism. It might be found in some forms of Buddhism, too (P. Harvey 2019). Scholars have found a kind of idle creator God (*deus otiosus*) in some African religions, although Western conceptual import has historically misconstrued the precise nature of these beliefs (Westerlund 1985). Other examples, including the Bahā'ī faith, the Druze, or the Maasai religion, may be given (Westerlund 2006).

The main difficulty with any definition of monotheism is that 'god' is notoriously hard to define (West 1999). The moment one seeks to define monotheism and use it comparatively, one runs into the tension between internal and external perspectives since there is no universal agreement about what we mean by 'god'. What might, for some insiders, look like a subordinate created being – a cherub, for example – might, for outsiders, be defined as a divine being. Hence, from a comparative perspective, one might even begin to ask whether the Abrahamic religions are truly monotheistic, given the plethora of divine councils, angels, powers, and messengers testified to in their scriptures.

It should not be surprising that Jan Assmann concludes that as 'an instrument for describing and classifying ancient religions, the opposition of unity and plurality is practically worthless' (Assmann 2010, 31). Indeed, not only is the term 'god' highly contested, but the meaning of God's *oneness* is far from obvious. Influential theological traditions in Christianity, Islam, and Judaism have insisted that the notion of the oneness of God does not mean that the set of all gods has only one instance. The idea of thinking about God's oneness as a numerical issue causes difficulties for many monotheistic traditions, which are cautious about making God a member of a set.

The difficulty with defining monotheism arises because one cannot describe the position in question (monotheism) without oneself staking a position. That is why, in discussions about monotheism, 'semantic antinomies' tend to arise (Colpe 2007, 23). On the one hand, monotheism cannot be sufficiently defined without presupposing at least some basic ontological parameters, yet, on the other, monotheisms themselves arise as basic ontological construals of the world. Monotheistic religions disagree about the metaphysical sense of the claim that God is one, but there seems to be no way of defining monotheism without staking at least some metaphysical ground, and thus taking a conceptual position on the meaning of the word 'god' and its relationship to other concepts.

In making this claim, I stake my own ground: I believe that monotheistic theologies inevitably make decisions about questions of being, unity, and multiplicity. On the level of definition, Debra Scoggins Ballentine rightly points out that 'the term monotheism is imprecise, not in etymology, but in conceptualization' (Ballentine 2022, 4). I submit that conceptualisation is impossible without metaphysical clarification about the relationship between the absolute and the relative, the transcendent and the immanent, or God and creation. Thus, the assertion that there is one God is not primarily about how many are in the set of gods. Instead, with monotheism, we are dealing, in the words of David Bentley Hart, with a distinction 'between two entirely different kinds of reality, belonging to two entirely disparate conceptual orders' (Hart 2013, 29). The belief in the One True God is not to do with an entity in the world, something describable as a neatly defined object among others in the universe of discourse. Instead, it is a confession to the 'infinite source of all things', the absolute truth that is at once transcendent and immanent to all things (Hart 2013, 30). Despite its highly speculative nature, I think some formula of this sort is implied by the confession that God is the absolute truth. For that very reason, however, any description of the 'one' God requires a clarification not only of this distinction between the 'disparate conceptual orders' but also of their relationship.

Another difficulty attending to any consideration of the politics of monotheism is that the notion of monotheism is politicised as such. The most important origin of the concept is, of course, in the religious cultures of the Abrahamic traditions. However, the notion of Abrahamic religions is itself a brittle construction, rising out of religious negotiations, dialogue, and projection. The phrase was seldom used until recent times. In modern times, monotheism has functioned as a unifying term for the religious traditions of Islam, Christianity, and Judaism. Yet, it has also served as part of an attempt at differentiation – as with Islamic criticisms of Christian theology for being insufficiently monotheistic. It is used by anti-colonial critics of Western powers, Islamist terrorists, defenders of the universal validity of human rights, and ideologues of the US interventions in Afghanistan and Iraq.

There might be no consensus on the definition of monotheism, yet why is it so politically charged? Monotheism is associated both with universalism and particularism and exhibits the aporias of these categories in modern social and political life. The one God is the God of all, the One who concerns each individual individually, as St Augustine saw. The belief in the One God may challenge any presumption of exclusivity; it may justify a universal ethic of love, justice, or respect – as Mahatma Gandhi and many others have thought – and may cast suspicion on every worldly authority (Gandhi 2009). However, the One God may also divide the world into two: between God and evil, the existent and the non-existent, the elected and the unelected. The rejection of idolatry and monotheistic notions of revelation introduces this distinction. The idea of idolatry erects a distinction between the true God and false imitations of Him, and revelation mediates knowledge of this distinction to human beings – or even creates, through a covenant – the subject that can stand on the right side of this distinction. If a singular or localised expression, people, or event comes to be understood as the only legitimate expression of human response to the One God – as in John Calvin's 'godly' Geneva – then one can imagine how monotheism may contribute to a politics based on exclusion and antagonism (Naphy 2003).

Even as monotheism is associated with such opposite tendencies, it is a matter of dispute what grounds such relationships between monotheism and politics. I venture to show that monotheism is politically significant because it configures human relationships to truth and because Western political life has a particularly fraught relationship with the truth. In this Element, then, I will focus on the relationship between monotheism, politics, and truth in a Western and primarily Christian context. My aim is not to evaluate the effect of mono-theism globally or throughout history. Rather, I want to take my point of departure with ideas about monotheism as they have been received and debated in modern cultures influenced by the traditions of Christianity. This is not, however, because I think the issue of the politics of monotheism can be 'resolved' only from a Christian context, but rather because I am wary of how certain Western experiences have been solidified and projected beyond their context. Part of my contribution to the discussion about monotheism's political consequences, then, is reframing the issue in light of two interrelated historical and intellectual transitions in European history.

First, many of the contemporary debates arose from the difficult relationship between politics and truth in modern societies influenced by the early modern history of Europe. 'Monotheism' as a term arose precisely when European political life had been upset by the theologico-political tumults after the Reformation that provoked a reconsideration between politics and truth. The two seemingly opposite tendencies of monotheism – universality and exclusion – reflect some deep-seated tendencies within modern Western politics. The breakup of the Holy Roman Empire and the division of Europe into a multitude of different religious confessions led to attempts to bracket truth – or certain truth claims – from politics. This stirred a search for new universals, governed by the idea that a dogmatic confession to religious truth would drive conflict in the political realm. Given such a history, it is impossible to consider monotheism and politics as two separate issues. Instead, we must consider them as part of a complex theologico-political complex with a deep history that still informs our contemporary dilemmas and debates.

Second, within these complicated transitions in European modernity, some deep metaphysical relationships were being reconfigured. As I understand it, monotheism entails the belief in a God who is the absolute truth. It is a truth that cannot be explained or subsumed to another, higher perspective. Absolute truth seems to be something that cannot be shared or translated – it is unrepeatable. However, it is precisely this impossibility of translating and sharing the truth that makes monotheism seem so problematic, and it is why Jan Assmann claims that monotheism *is* the Mosaic distinction, the division between those who confess the absolute truth and those who do not. The problem with monotheism is that it seems to draw a strict line between true and false religion, which may turn into a distinction between friend and enemy in the political realm, should we believe Assmann. Ever since the Enlightenment, Western thinkers have been deeply worried about this dynamic. In *The Critique of Pure Reason*, Immanuel Kant noted the need for a critique of reason, a deduction and delineation of the categories and limits of reason precisely because he worried about the antagonisms of religious truth (Kant 1998; DiCenso 2011). For him, metaphysics was a history of violence because there was no accepted authority on which to settle disputes. That view of history was novel but has become commonplace in European intellectual life.

However, I venture that the early modern European experience has shaped Western categories of religion and monotheism to such an extent that they skew and misrepresent significant aspects of monotheistic traditions. Assmann and Kant assume a distinction between God and creation that is far from obvious in major monotheistic traditions. The instance of Kant is illuminating: his way of ensuring that confessions to absolute truth are kept at a safe distance from political life depends on another set of distinctions: that between faith and knowledge, the transcendental and the empirical, and the noumenal and the phenomenal. In other words: there is a widespread tendency among modern European thinkers of the relationship between religion and politics to establish a dichotomy between the absolute and the relative, the transcendent and the immanent, or God and creation. Only thus can there be a domain shielded from monotheism's confession to the absolute truth.

I believe, however, that this assumed solution to the ambivalent politics of monotheism itself contributes to framing monotheism in such a way that it can only ever be abstractly universal or antagonistic when allowed in political life. Either the worship of the one God belongs to a domain of religious truth separate from secular political life (at best only indirectly in touch with politics through the domain of universal 'values'), or religious truth enters the secular domain from the outside in a totalitarian and divisive fashion. Such a way of framing the issue is only possible if one has already construed the relationship between the divine and the created order in a way that diverges from significant monotheistic traditions.

My claim is that it is impossible to correctly understand the confession to absolute truth in monotheistic traditions without recognising that it depends on settling the relationship between the absolute and the relative, or God and creation. If one is, for example, to say that pledging allegiance to a particular ruler is a form of idolatry, that the nation-state demands an idolatrous sacrifice of its people (Cavanaugh 2004), or that capitalism represents the 'enchantments of Mammon' (McCarraher 2019), one needs a particular understanding of precisely how God relates to creation. Otherwise, it makes no sense to say that something or someone is transgressing its proper place as a finite being or that relative truth is taken for absolute truth.

However, this relationship between God and creation is not something one can take for granted. Contrary to the hopes of many modern thinkers, it is precisely *not* established for all times and places by universal reason, but something that believers – and theologians – in monotheistic traditions have negotiated all the time, informed by what they thought it meant to represent God faithfully. This liminal space between God and creation is both fiercely guarded and highly porous in monotheistic thought and practice. It follows from the very confession that God is the absolute truth that God cannot just be 'different' from creation in the way things are 'different' within creation itself.

Thus, while the notion of idolatry is crucial to understanding the political legacy of monotheism, we must pay attention to not only the distinction between true and false gods but also the prohibition against images. This prohibition has an enormous influence on how Judaism, Christianity, and Islam have thought about God's relationship to created things and, in particular, to what extent God may be represented, imitated, or mirrored. However, where Assmann understands this prohibition as absolute, I believe monotheism is best understood if we acknowledge that the ban against images creates a wide variety ways to question limits and possibilities of how the divine might be represented, with the aniconic position (the total ban) being only one position in a broader spectrum. As we add this axis of representation to the picture, we cannot define monotheism as a pure distinction between true and false religion, as per Assmann. Once we see that the total ban is only one position among many in monotheistic traditions, we can see that monotheisms often think of absolute truth as something that may be *shared*, something that created realities may partake in and reflect in specific ways.

When we approach the topic of the ban against images, we approach the issue of representation. Debates about the politics of monotheism may sometimes be framed in terms of what sort of effects certain *ideas* about God might have in politics, directly or indirectly. This is to treat monotheism as a set of religious truth claims that may have beneficial or detrimental effects. However, important monotheistic traditions, including Christianity, put significant pressure on any truth claims about God, including the claim that God is 'one'. For that reason, practices of critique, refinement, and disavowal of representation are internal to monotheism. Such practices do not, however, belong to an entirely separate 'religious' sphere of culture, but are 'internal' to or intertwined with major Western political traditions – and are ultimately caught up with what it means to 'represent' in political life as well.[3]

Thus, what I want to argue in this Element is not that there is a single 'politics of monotheism' or that all monotheistic religions are equal to the extent that they are monotheistic. I use the term *descriptively* as the confession to One God, who is the absolute Truth, but I am doubtful about its value as a generalised term of *explanation*. Rather than asking about the political effects of monotheism, understood as a representation of religious truth, I am interested in the *politics* of representation in monotheistic traditions.

I shall argue that because many of the recent critiques of monotheism have inherited a problematic view of religion, they circumvent the discussion of the relationship between the absolute and the relative, the transcendent and the immanent. In so doing, they bracket the complex negotiation between God and creation in monotheistic traditions, and so the issue of representation. Instead, they assume a general critique or worry about representation as such – they explicitly or implicitly identify any representation of the One God as incipiently violent. In other words, the critique of monotheism draws it force from the Enlightenment worry about any religious representation of the absolute.

While much of this Element will be spent trying to establish that claim, I also make some initial suggestions about how a certain kind of monotheism might negotiate its relationship to truth. In this case, I will work with ideas and debates from the traditions of Christian truth, which are the ones I, as a Christian theologian, tend to work with. In this tradition, the idea that God has become incarnate in Jesus Christ that both modifies Jewish monotheism and raises the stakes in how one is to represent the One God.

To discuss the question of representation in this manner is not to leave the topic of the 'politics of monotheism' but to interrogate an essential aspect of it.

---

[3] For some key works that are attentive to the religious background of Western ideas of political representation, see Pitkin (1967); Vieira and Runciman (2008).

Thus, I believe Nancy is correct that Western societies struggle with their relationship to truth. Still, I also believe that theses about the 'clash of civilisations' and the fear of the influence of monotheism on political life depends on a construction of our relationship to truth that significant monotheistic traditions do not necessarily share.

Thus, I cannot offer a universal theory of the politics of monotheism, nor is that my concern. What I can do, from within the tradition of Christian thought, is to show how a kind of monotheism may negotiate its relationship to truth. In particular, I will assess some Christian critics of monotheism and discuss how the Christian belief in the incarnation affects the notion of idolatry in Christian theology. In so doing, I suggest that approaching the 'politics of monotheism' as a question of whether a certain kind of cognitive assent to the existence of one God may have beneficial or detrimental consequences is wrongheaded. I do not seek to excuse monotheism but to bring back focus to the concrete negotiations of divine truth and human life that have informed and been reformed in those religious traditions we commonly call monotheistic.

In the first section of this Element, I present Jan Assmann's theory of the Mosaic distinction, a highly influential theory about the political significance of monotheism. In the second and third sections, I seek to contextualise and qualify Assmann's approach by indicating the historical conditions of Western ideas about religion and monotheism, drawing on recent critical research on religion. In the fourth section, I turn to some Christian thinkers who have sought to criticise monotheism and its political consequences from the vantage points of the doctrine of the Trinity. From this discussion, I move to discuss the relevance of the Christian doctrine of the incarnation for the politics of monotheism and show the significance of the issues of representation and idolatry in the Christian politics of monotheism. In the final section, I sum up the Element and make some suggestions about how we can think about the politics of monotheism and the representation of absolute truth in political life, without indulging in reductive theories about monotheism as something inherently good or bad.

2 The Mosaic Distinction

In the decades around the turn of the millennium, monotheism became a focal point for a series of debates, including issues of violence, terrorism, nationalism, human rights, and globalisation. The old imperial ghosts of Christendom and Islamic empires were revived, and commentators worried that we were seeing a competition between Christian and Islamic monotheisms played out in an international political context. Among the academics who wrote significant works on monotheism, politics, and violence was Jan Assmann, a German

Egyptologist and specialist on the history of memory.[4] Assmann claimed that monotheism, as traditioned and transformed in the religious traditions that trace their origins to Abraham and Moses, harbours an exceptional potential for violence. For him, monotheism's claim to absolute truth is potentially problematic when carried over into politics. Assmann's view of monotheism was nuanced and did not deny the beneficial aspects of monotheism. Still, it did leave the impression that monotheism had extraordinary potential for conflict and had to be approached carefully lest it have detrimental effects on political life. In this section, I will explain Assmann's thesis and how it portrayed monotheism's relationship to truth and its political ramifications. I will suggest that our received understanding of monotheism is fundamentally shaped by a series of narratives of concepts received from the religious and political conflicts of early modernity, which I will unpack in the following section.

Monotheism introduces a distinction between true and false religion. That is the core of Jan Assmann's well-known thesis, which he set forth in the work *Moses the Egyptian* (1998).[5] Monotheism, in this sense, is not an assent to numerical unity but the claim that 'alongside the One True God, there are only false gods, whom it is strictly forbidden to worship' (Assmann 2010, 34). This 'Mosaic distinction' multiplies and divides the religious space: 'Jews and Gentiles, Christians and pagans, Muslims and unbelievers', and then 'Catholics and Protestants, Calvinists and Lutherans, Socinians and Latidudinarians', and so forth (Assmann 1997, 1). Distinctions create and stabilise meaning and identity but also contribute to a universe 'full of conflict, intolerance, and violence'. In contrast to monotheism, polytheistic cultures have logics of 'translation', according to Assmann (Assmann 1997, 2–3). Without the Mosaic distinction, it is possible to recognise that other peoples have other gods than our own, yet also acknowledge that these gods play corresponding roles, as do ours. Monotheism rejects the very possibility of translation and thus a kind of recognition that encourages tolerance.

Although, according to Assmann, monotheism was introduced by the Egyptian pharaoh Akhenaten in the fourteenth century BCE, it was the memory of Moses that ensured that the monotheistic world view would form the world of 'Europeans for nearly two millennia' (Assmann 1997, 2). According to this memory, which runs through the variegated sediments of the monotheistic

---

[4] Another prominent critic was Regina Schwartz, who, in *Curse of Cain: The Violent Legacy of Monotheism* (1997), used the story of Cain and Abel as a sypher for understanding monotheism's contribution to the construction of identity a negative or antagonistic logic. Schwartz was writing from a background in literature, and focused on the narrative repertoire of monotheistic traditions. See Schwartz (1997). Still other critics include Sloterdijk (2009). An older critique was set forth by Odo Marquard in Marquard (1989).

[5] See Assmann (1997). Originally published as Assmann (1998)

traditions, building on the stories of Moses, Egypt 'symbolizes what is rejected, discarded, and abandoned', he claims. In the Mosaic traditions, Egypt represents slavery and idolatry. The people of Israel had to be saved from Egypt, and Egypt as a religious culture is rejected by the first commandment:[6]

> I am the Lord your God, who brought you out of the land of Egypt, out of the house of slavery; you shall have no other gods before me. You shall not make for yourself an idol, whether in the form of anything that is in heaven above, or that is on the earth beneath, or that is in the water under the earth. You shall not bow down to them or worship them; for I the Lord your God am a jealous God, punishing children for the iniquity of parents, to the third and the fourth generation of those who reject me, but showing steadfast love to the thousandth generation of those who love me and keep my commandments. (Exodus 20:1–6)

Even if Israelite religion was pluriform, one of the 'voices' arising from the texts in the Hebrew Bible is those from Deuteronomy and Deutero-Isaiah, which claimed sole worship of Yahweh and forbade the worship of other gods, who were deemed false (Assmann 2010, 34). There are many aspects one might associate with Mosaic monotheism, including the worship of the One God, the notion of an election and covenant, and the notion of revelation. For Assmann, however, none of these notions is as fundamental to his understanding of monotheism as the Mosaic distinction since it is only through the distinction between true and false religion that these aspects are understood antagonistically. In this sense, monotheism attempts to establish a clean 'break with the past' and generates religious difference and antagonism, 'manifesting itself in countless acts of violence and bloodshed' (Assmann 2010, 11). As Assmann has broadened his argument from the Mosaic tradition, he has argued that all major 'world religions' are Mosaic in this sense of erecting an unequivocal distinction between truth and falsehood.

Assmann investigates the politics of monotheism in history and memory. Biblical monotheism is a memory with questionable historical founding (Moses and the exodus from Egypt) but with a long and effective history, which includes vast consequences for political life. One of Assmann's main goals of *Moses the Egyptian* was to trace the memory of Moses in early modern Europe and in Enlightenment discourse in particular. Assmann is especially interested in the European 'Egyptomania' from the middle of the seventeenth century to the time of Napoleon, during which Egypt was understood as background and in contrast to monotheism (Assmann 1997, 19). He notes that the interest was kindled by the religio-political conflict of the time, though he does not develop that context further.

---

[6] See Assmann (1997, 209).

In this European tradition, Moses was surprisingly portrayed as an Egyptian, thus 'abolishing this defining opposition' between idolatrous Egypt and the 'counter-religion' of Moses (Assmann 1997, 168). Whereas the old Judeo-Christian binary understood Moses in terms of unity and Egypt in terms of plurality, the new binary traced unity itself back to Egypt. Here, the Enlightenment religion of reason was attributed to Egypt, and Moses' monotheism was understood as a political or civil theology in the Roman scholar Varro's (116–27 BCE) sense: as a public legitim-ation of power, which nonetheless hides the real religious mysteries of the elites (Pépin 1956). In this discursive tradition, monotheism was understood as harbour-ing a logic of repressive authority – which Freud later theorised as fatherhood. Interestingly, Assmann follows parts of this tradition, identifying monotheism as a 'counter-religion': It rejects the Egyptian polytheism and is a 'secondary religion' which it arises through (textual) reflection on and rejection of 'primary religion', understood as an immediate and pre-reflexive presupposition of the human condition.

The Amarna religion, founded by Akhenaten as a striking exception in Egyptian history, was 'cosmotheistic', rationalistic, disenchanting, and anti-sacramental (Assmann 1997, 169–70). Biblical monotheism – understood as a theological construct, not as a lived religion – feeds off the rejection of polytheistic Egypt and is fiercely anti-idolatrous. Assmann claims that the rejection of false gods determined the prohibition against images, and that images are 'automatically "other gods," because the true god is invisible and cannot be represented' (Assmann 1997, 4). Politically speaking, the ban on images 'destroys the sphere of representation in which the state legitimizes itself (or purports to legitimize itself) as a church, as the earthly presence of the divine; and it disenchants the world, which otherwise casts a spell on man and turns him away from god'. Monotheism is, in short, against every form of representation of the divine (Assmann 2010, 70).

For Assmann, the appearance of monotheism introduces a reordering of the categories of religion and politics. This transition, or difference, between cos-motheism and monotheism is quite complex: since there was no absolute divine transcendence in cosmotheism, it did not make sense to appeal to an absolute truth against, say, a particular king. The ruler was divine and provided 'the link between the divine world and human society' (Assmann 2016, 9). The divine as such was simply the architecture of, and so immanent to, to the cosmos. There was, then, no explicit differentiation between social order and religion (understood as a way of relating to absolute truth), and thus no sense of a higher 'religion' to appeal to. Yet, there was a distinction between justice on the one hand and cult – the rituals of sacrifice and mediation with the gods – on the other. Thus, whereas, on the broadest, symbolic or 'invisible' level, everything in cosmotheistic society was 'religious'; on the 'visible' or institutional level, 'religion' was restricted to the cult, and had essentially nothing to do with justice:

> Whereas the gods crave sacrificial offerings, humans crave the law. In its origins, justice is something profane or secular. Religion and ethics have different roots, and in primary religions they constitute separate, albeit inter-connected, spheres. Only in monotheism are they fused into an inseparable unity. (Assmann 2010, 50)

What then, should we make of this claim, that monotheism represents a fusion of cult and justice? Assmann believes that monotheism introduced a distinction between absolute truth and human truth, putting salvation firmly in the hand of God (Assmann 2010, 47). After monotheism, 'religion and politics are two different things' (Assmann 2010, 46). It thus became possible to appeal to 'religion' against 'politics', in that any political ruler could be challenged from the perspective of divine truth.

Because of that differentiation, however, monotheism allows for a novel fusion of religion and politics – on several interconnected levels. First, as noted in the previous quote, it 'annuls the distinction' between 'cult' and 'justice', so that the whole of life is potentially subordinated to a religion that demands, not only sacrifice, but justice. 'The concept of justice thereby ceases to found a sphere that exists outside of specific relations with the divine' (Assmann 2014, 173). Second, it transfers 'profane' ideas that originally belonged to ethics or politics into the domain of religion. The ban on idolatry is precisely such an example, since it demands allegiance to God as the only, unquestionable ruler. Third, it allows, for the first time, a 'forced union' between religion and politics, in that it is now possible to appeal to 'religion' to legitim-ate the state (Assmann 2010, 48).

This novel potential for fusion between religion and politics is a consequence of monotheism's notion of absolute truth. The Mosaic distinction establishes an absolute distinction between truth and falsity and demands submission to the former. When this distinction is introduced or repeated in the political sphere, it has the potential to channel antagonistic passions and promote exclusionary mechanisms. For monotheistic religions, 'the truth to be proclaimed comes with an enemy to be fought' (Assmann 2010, 4). Yet, how, exactly, does the Mosaic distinction enter political life, and what is its inherent danger?

In an essay, Assmann employs the German legal theorist Carl Schmitt's (1888–1985) concept of the political to connect monotheism and politics. Assmann grants that the belief in absolute truth does not, on its own, explain the violent potential of monotheism; he also needs a theory of the relationship between truth and violence, and he looks to Schmitt to account for this link

(Assmann 2016, 113). He refers to Schmitt's idea of a state of emergency (*Ernstfall*), a limit-situation in which the political nature of the state moves into the foreground.[7] According to Schmitt, who became the infamous 'Kronjurist' of the Third Reich, in a state of emergency, as in a war, the true ground of political association appears as the distinction between friend and enemy.[8] This political distinction between friend and enemy does not so much establish a separate realm as it surpasses every other distinction or cultural sphere.[9] In the state of exception, every aspect of life can be mobilised and framed by the antagonistic relationship between friend and enemy, which is why Assmann understands Schmitt's concept of the political as a totalisation of politics: Schmitt 'wants the whole human being, the united people, the total state' (Assmann 2016, 116). The distinction between friend and enemy is absolute; it leaves no space for neutrality and forces every person to take sides.

Assmann claims that monotheism enables a similar 'religious' totalisation. In the Jewish tradition, the notions of covenant and apocalyptic revelation are the foundational cases of religious *Ernstfall*, associating a people into a community against a common enemy, thereby raising 'a totalizing claim, requiring hegemony over all the domains of culture' (Assmann 2016, 123). Judaism is unique in that the Mosaic distinction leads primarily to an exclusivist and particularistic response so that violence is directed inwards. Nevertheless, the apocalyptic moment, in which the human life is forced to takes side in a divine drama, comes to the fore with Christianity and Islam because their missional and universalist tendencies transpose the distinction into a cosmic key (Assmann 2016, 124). These religions universalise the distinction to apply to everyone so that they 'explode into violence' when followers of these religions translate absolute truth into an absolute political distinction between friend and enemy (Assmann 2010, 18).

Assmann does not merely use the friend–enemy distinction as an analogy; his comparison contains a historical claim. The Mosaic distinction is, we learn, originally a political distinction transformed into the distinction between true and false worship. Political violence, which depends on a distinction between friend and foe, is the origin of religious violence, though only dialectically: religious violence in the monotheistic sense is, originally, a violence pitted against political violence (Assmann 2008, 143–45) Similarly, other aspects of monotheism, such as that of the covenant, are products of transference from a political to a religious sphere: 'We are dealing with the transposition of an

---

[7] The subject of the state of exception was discussed in the influential work (Schmitt 2005).

[8] For the definitive biography of Schmitt's life, including his relationship to Nazism, see Mehring (2014).

[9] Schmitt developed this distinction between friend and enemy in Schmitt (2007).

originally political concept to the religious level, transforming god–king, king–subject, and king–vassal relations into the relations between god and man as well as God and Israel' (Assmann 2016, 119). This transposition also included an inversion since Israel's covenant is the covenant of liberation where '[l]oyalty becomes fidelity, vassaldom becomes covenant, and politics becomes religion'.

Assmann seems to think that monotheism represents a questionable or even illegitimate transfer from politics to religion so that monotheism is an odd form of religion, a 'counter-religion' that exhibits a potentially violent political logic. As such, the transference from politics to religion might have functioned as a way of desacralising the politics of the imperial powers of the Near East since, now, the symbolic frame of justification of political rulers appears as poor imitations of Israel's covenant with God. Paradoxically, however, this transference opens the possibility of channelling an entirely new form of antagonism; when these concepts return to the political sphere, they begin to operate according to the antagonistic relation produced by the Mosaic distinction. Therefore, in *Herrschaft und Heil: Politische Theologie in Altägypten, Israel und Europa*, Assmann writes that a political theology of violence 'consists in the theologisation of the distinction between friend and enemy' where the 'enemy becomes declared a divine enemy' (Assmann 2000, 25).[10]

With this analysis of Schmitt and with the conclusion that monotheism represents a questionable fusion of the realm of violence (politics) with the realm of cult and cosmology (religion), I need to make some initial critical remarks. I am not the first to do so since Assmann's work has given rise to a considerable and complex debate – especially in Germany, where it has been referred to as the 'monotheism debate' (Schieder 2014). Some scholars, for example, have argued that he overplays the Mosaic distinction and underplays the presence of translatability in biblical traditions (M. S. Smith 2010). Others have challenged his rejection of the Mosaic distinction itself. Several scholars agree with Mark S. Smith that 'the ancient correlations that Assmann posits between monotheism and violence, between translatability of divinity and tolerance, hardly hold up to scrutiny' (Schieder 2008; Hart 2009; Smith 2010, 326). Conversely, the idea that polytheism does not 'theologically' sanction violence is also disputable.

In *The Price of Monotheism* (2003), Assmann responded to his critics and underscored that he did not think of monotheism as entirely regrettable but only to understand its meaning and effects.[11] He accepts that monotheism did not bring violence into the world and admits that it may have had beneficial effects. But he also argues that 'this kind of religion implies a new type of violence'

---

[10] My translation.   [11] See Assmann (2010). Originally published as Assmann (2003).

(Assmann 2005, 141–42). Monotheism introduces a truth that is 'absolute, revealed, metaphysical, or fideistic' (Assmann 2010, 15).

One must ask, however, where exactly monotheism exists according to Assmann's approach. He openly admits that his notion of monotheism does not coincide with the broad religious traditions and histories we usually think of as monotheistic. At one point, he claims that one might talk about 'monotheistic moments' when the Mosaic distinction is most evident, even if it recedes into the background and fades into the compromises and complexities of everyday life (Assmann 2010, 2–3). Monotheism does not, then, actually refer to a whole religious tradition, such as Judaism or Christianity, which would include all the complexities of belief, practice, and ritual of this tradition. The Mosaic distinction is 'the melody sung by a particular voice, not the refrain of a permanently established religion' (Assmann 2010, 34). Thus, the theologies related to the Mosaic distinction in the Old Testament do not overlap in its entirety with the religious history of Israel (Assmann 2010, 33). He, therefore, claims that counterexamples – religious practices where the Mosaic distinction makes no difference – are no problem for him (Assmann 2010, 33).

At times, Assmann speaks of monotheism, or 'secondary religion', as a kind of ideal type – a theological idea' that might or might not be present in a concrete religion at some point in time (Assmann 2010, 34). He claims that while the ban against worshipping other Gods is a 'leading idea in all three of the so-called Abrahamic religions', the notion of monotheism as a counter-religion 'does not refer to any specific religion existing in historical reality but rather to a theoretical construct or model, like Max Weber's "ideal type," which may be more or less adequately applied to various historical phenomena' (Assmann 2008, 110).

It is not entirely clear that Assmann is speaking of an ideal type in an ordinary sense. An ideal type is a heuristic device that highlights certain common features among varied phenomena, without treating them as expressions of an underlying essence. It is an epistemological, not an ontological category. However, Assmann's distinction between 'primary' and 'secondary' religions is not really a distinction between two ideal types (as between 'liberal' or 'conservative' in a political context) that may or may not be present at various points in historical reality. It is, in fact, a distinction between a primary pre-reflexive level of religious practice and secondary reflective theology that seeks a high level of purity. It is monotheism, in particular, that is *essentially* ideal-typical; it is, in other words, a kind of striving for a purity that can, by definition, almost never be attained in real life. Monotheism is *essentially* an abstract 'regulative idea' set in opposition to the complexity of concrete religious practice, which, from the perspective of mono-theism, is designated as 'polytheism' (Assmann 2010, 35). Yet, while the Mosaic distinction is a theological rather than religious affair, and while monotheism can only portray its opposite as a competing theology of 'polytheism', primary religion actually is not striving for idealistic or doctrinal purity in this sense (Assmann 2010, 35). In fact, 'primary religion' is just 'religion' in a general sense; it belongs to the 'basic conditions of human existence' (Steinmetz-Jenkins 2011, 515).

Thus, we are not speaking about 'distinct features' that are muddied up together in real life, but more precisely a particular kind of intention (monotheism) that strives for purity, even if it is actually tied into a wide variety of impure practices we would associate with primary religion. If we think of monotheism as an actually existing religion, it is, of course, impure. But monotheism as a theology seeks absolute purity. For this reason, Assmann's theory of monotheism implies a theory of false consciousness: Egypt is the repressed other of monotheism; primary religion is the 'erased text' of the manuscript on which 'counter-religion' has inscribed itself (Assmann 1997, 209). The 'pagan' origins of mono-theism 'has to be forgotten and made invisible', which means that secondary religion develops 'a new form of unconsciousness' (Assmann 2010, 109).

Now, this theory of repression indicates why monotheism cannot just be an ideal type for Assmann: One would not propose a theory of repression for an ideal type. A politician who is a bit conservative as well as a bit liberal is not necessarily deluding herself; she just does not entirely fit the ideal types. By contrast, only if there is such a thing called monotheism, most visible at certain points in history, that seeks a high level of purity, could one speak of it as being deluded or expressing a kind of false consciousness.

Thus, we must ask why Assmann points to this theoretical construct, this idea that 'only attained to the dignity of an idea in the modern age', as the definition of monotheism? To what extent may the persistence of this propensity towards a pure counter-religion be thought of as a primary signifier of these traditions (Markschies 2010)? Put in other terms, why should complex phenomena in which there are various layers of religiousness and practice be described as evidence of failed attempts at purity – why postulate this intention for absolute purity (the Mosaic distinction), use it as a term for the whole complex of practices (mono-theism as a lived religion), and then claim that it bears a false consciousness? Why not, instead, take the complexity as evidence that 'monotheism' is not necessarily best described as such by such attempts at absolute purity?

Another issue, however, concerns Assmann's definition of religion and polit-ics. Assmann operates with a universalist, trans-historical definition of religion, paying little attention to the critiques of the category of religion written since the 1990s.[12] Such critiques challenge some of the dichotomies that Assmann

---

[12] This field is now well known, and several important works were written before Assmann's work on monotheism. Some key works include Balagangadhara (1994); Smith (1998); Connolly

employs by historicising them in the early modern European theologico-political experience. Thus, we must ask how the modern categories of religion, politics, and political theology shape Assmann's argument and his understanding of monotheism.

In the next sections, I would like to suggest that there is a duplicity in Assmann's argument that ought to be understood in light of certain developments in European modernity. On the one hand, Assmann claims that monotheistic religions harbour a dangerous potential for violence. Because they confess absolute truth and demand unconditional submission to this truth, and because they mix this religious demand with politics, they have a hazardous potential for violence. On the other hand, Assmann claims that religion is essentially peaceable and non-political. As I shall seek to explain, these claims are not contradictory but rather express an ambivalence inscribed in the modern concept of religion Assmann employs. Assmann argues that the memory of the Mosaic distinction originates in the Old Testament texts and is only challenged and modified in early European modernity. I shall argue that we should also take the opposite chronology into account: that the understanding of monotheism Assmann employs can be understood as a product of early modern and Enlightenment thinking. Even if we grant that the idea of monotheism is not a complete anachronism, I believe we must question some of the later Enlightenment approaches to monotheism and politics that Assmann presumes.

3 Monotheism in the Conflicts of Modern Europe

Contemporary debates about monotheism are inflected with categories, narratives, and ideas inherited from the theologico-political transformations that occurred in early modern Europe. These events shaped and introduced some fundamental views of religion and politics that we continue to grapple with today.[13] In particular, these transformations introduced into modern social imaginaries (the socio-symbolic 'context' of thought and action) a clear distinction between the transcendent and the immanent spheres of human existence. I submit that we can only understand the politics of monotheism if we understand and reflect on that background. In the following, I will outline some significant developments in modern European conceptions of religion and politics as they relate to the politics of monotheism before I discuss how this picture relates to Assmann's thesis about monotheism.

(1999); King (1999); Asad (2003); Masuzawa (2005); Dubuisson (2007); McCutcheon (2007); Fitzgerald (2007b); Cavanaugh (2009); Nongbri (2013); Mahmood (2016).

[13] I have discussed some general aspects of this legacy at length in Bergem (2019).

Before the Enlightenment, Christian cultures operated with a fourfold classification of *religio*: Alongside Christianity were its relatives Judaism and Islam, outside which were the heathens – a term that essentially included everything else.[14] This, however, was not a classification of religion in the modern sense. In the Christian Middle Ages, 'religio' referred to a virtue of devotion and prayer, and its established Roman meaning also included the broader, but very concrete sense of fulfilling one's ritual duties (Feil 1992; Harrison 2017, 7). Nonetheless, religion was not a universal of which Christianity or Islam were particulars; *religio* was not a category in the way that modern Europeans came to use it. Christians could, of course, position themselves in relation to Muslims or Manicheans, but they did so without the category of religion. Christians recognised a connection with Judaism and Islam, even if that connection was framed in largely polemical terms. Judaism and Islam could be viewed as ancestors and offspring, yet also as internal and external enemies. Yet, until modern times, Christians did not use the term 'monotheism'. The oneness, or 'monarchy' of God, was, of course, a notion shared among Christians, Jews, and Muslims, but it was also a concept of dispute.

By the time of the Reformation, this fourfold differentiation of *religio* was still in use. Yet, when the term 'monotheism' first appeared in early modern Europe, the notion of religion was beginning to be understood in new ways. In recent decades, scholars have sought to trace the construction of the modern category of religion and have emphasised the colonial context as a key origin. These scholars point out that the notion that religion represents a distinct sphere of human life and thought, one that can also be distinguished from politics, is far from obvious and that it is a peculiarity of modern Europeans to have begun to think of religion in this way. The study of religion grew out of the recognition that the world was much more complex than what could be captured by a distinction between Christians and heathens. Furthermore, as we will see presently, other political developments strongly influenced the understanding of religion and monotheism.

The modern sense of religion as a universal human phenomenon is sometimes traced back to the Renaissance thinkers like Nicholas of Cusa (1401–65), Pico della Mirandola (1463–94), and Marsilio Ficino (1433–99), who were searching for a universal theology common to all faiths. Whereas Assmann believes that these thinkers sought to abolish the Mosaic distinction (Assmann 2010, 76–78), from another perspective, they represent a transmutation in a lineage of Christian and Platonist thought. Whether or not they thought of *religio* in quite a modern sense, they are part of a Christian lineage by which

---

[14] Before Islam, Christians had a threefold scheme: Massa (2017).

'natural theology', initially contrasted with revealed theology, became 'natural religion' in the early modern period. This occurs, according to Peter Byrne, 'when it is thought of not merely as a body of truths about God, but as so extensive a body of truths that it can generate a religion on its own' (Byrne 2015, 3). For Pico and others, Hebrew language and theology, as preserved in the Old Testament, were the most ancient and universal expressions of religion.

As Eric Nelson has argued, this 'Christian Hebraism' continued, in different forms, into the humanist strands of the Protestant Reformation (Nelson 2010). For the Protestant Hebraists, the Hebrew Republic came to be seen as the most perfect polity, having been founded by God himself. In this way, anti-Catholic hermeneutics, which stressed the independent value of the Old Testament, merged with a latent Platonic sense of a primal and universal theology and politics. Here, monotheism – or, more precisely, the monarchy of God – stood at the centre of an intellectual transformation of religion and politics.

Some reformers, notably the Lutheran Reformer Philipp Melanchthon (1497–1560), looked to the Decalogue as a foundational text for political rule (Berman 2003, 80). Interestingly, the reorientation to Israel as the standard for political rule by the Christian Hebraists, who were being informed by the reading of rabbinic sources, led to differing conclusions. In the seventeenth century, some theologians could argue that monarchy was a commandment from God, yet others that monarchy was a sin since it challenged God's status as the true monarch (Nelson 2010, 35–36). This latter interpretation, which represented a particular interpretation of monotheism in shocking contrast to the history of Christian justification of monarchy in the Middle Ages, contributed to the development of modern republican theory (Oakley 2006, 68–131; Kantorowicz 2016). The belief in God's singular rule could be used to challenge any earthly ruler who claimed absolute power for him or herself.

Arguments for toleration also grew out of this Christian Hebraism. In the sixteenth century, theologians such as Thomas Erastus (originally named 'Lüber') (1524–83) in Switzerland and Richard Hooker (1554–1600) in England noted that the ruler of Israel ordained both civil and religious laws, from which they drew an argument for an 'Erastian' fusion of ecclesiastic and political jurisdiction (Erastus 1682; Hooker 1989). However, they also developed a novel view that religious laws existed for the purpose of *civil* peace, thus giving them a temporal political justification. Alongside this argument, they recognised a distinction between private and public religion, acknowledging that private belief and observance concerned God alone.

A missing thread in Nelson's story is how the notion of religion itself developed, even if he touches upon what was essentially a new discourse about religion. He points to the Hebraism of Hugo Grotius (1583–1645), who also made a civic argument for regulating religion. In *Meletius* and *On the Rights of War and Peace*, Grotius wrote that there is a true religion common to all ages, whose precepts include the belief in One God, the distinction between God and the world, and God's concern for human beings (Grotius and Posthumus Meyjes 1988; Grotius and Tuck 2005, vol II, 1013). Grotius believed that these theological presuppositions were necessary for civic order. In this way, he turned a kind of minimal monotheism into a condition for political order, in a striking combination of Erastianism and universalism.

Such arguments tended to operate within a Christian tradition that distinguished between the Law and the Gospel and took for granted that there was a convergence between human reason and God's revealed law (Grotius and Tuck 2005, vol I, 179). We have seen that theologians could distinguish between private and public religion, yet these notions were still positioned within an explicitly Christian understanding of society. When Hooker, for example, argued for the civic usefulness of the belief in the One God, this was not a purely pragmatic argument but rather grounded in God's will for peace (Hooker 1989, 32, 186).

In contrast to the Christian Hebraists, the English deists of the seventeenth and eighteenth centuries focused not on the Old Testament but on religion as a phenomenon discoverable by reason and grounded in human nature (Byrne 2015, 8). Edward, Lord Herbert of Cherbury (1583–1648) was a forerunner of this idea (Feil 1992, 40–42). Some deists saw pure monotheism as a central doctrine in a universal and natural religion. The adjective 'Abrahamic' was first used in the 1730s, and the English deist Thomas Morgan (d. 1743), among others, used it to designate the universalist message of the three religious traditions (Silverstein, Stroumsa, and Silk 2015, 71). Yet, a writer such as Viscount Bolingbroke (1678–1751), who may have influenced later Enlightenment thinkers, thought that monotheism was discoverable by reason, present 'long before the commencement of traditions that we find out of the books of Moses' (Bolingbroke 1756, 2:165).

The invention of natural religion was politically inflected, for it was part of a recognition of religion as a *sui generis* phenomenon, which had significant political consequences. By 'sui generis', I mean that 'religion' came to be thought of as a sphere or a separable aspect of human life and came to work as a category with which concepts and things such as gods, cathedrals, baptism or faith might be associated. Although the discovery of new worlds through the colonial expansion and encounters by Western powers deeply contributed to such modern notions of religion, I think Niels Reeh is right that we should not underestimate the degree to which European concepts of religion were shaped by the Reformation and the so-called Wars of Religion, which lasted a roughly a century from the middle of the sixteenth century to the Peace of Westphalia in 1648, which ended the Thirty Years' War (Reeh 2020). He claims that our received concept(s) of religion arose as a result of the fact that 'war [...] necessitated the negotiation of peace treaties in which the parties recognized each other's practices in relation to their god as religion and not as heresy, infidelity, paganism, etc' (Reeh 2020, 98).

Reeh argues that the category of religion should itself be understood as a 'translatory' concept precisely in Assmann's sense: a concept that weakens the Mosaic distinction, allowing for a comparison of sameness and difference between religions. If the Christian understanding of *religio* was ultimately based on a definition of idolatry, which drew a line between Christianity and everything else, religion as a genus turned Christianity into one belief among others (even if it was deemed the true or supreme expression of religion). Being 'a concept and a domain that could be separated from the larger culture and society', religion could now 'be translated across religious borders' (Reeh 2020, 98).

Reeh claims that by locating this earlier source of the concept of religion, 'it follows that the notion of religion is not the result of the invention of scholars, philosophers, or thinkers as such' (Reeh 2020, 98). However, this is a non-sequitur. William Cavanaugh, Elizabeth Hurd, and others have argued that such variations of the 'Westphalian myth' of religious violence are best understood as elaborate attempts to construct the concept of religion and that this concept is often granted too much explanatory force to be of use to explain phenomena such as violence on a trans-historical scale (Fitzgerald 2007a; Hurd 2008; Cavanaugh 2009). Enlightenment narratives of the Wars of Religion have shaped our sense that religion is something that can be distinguished from political authority and even that it must be held separate from it. While religion in modern times came to be seen as a matter of individual, private belief, it also came to be understood as 'a major facet of any society', inevitably playing an ambivalent role in political life (Stroumsa 2010, 9).[15]

These understandings of religion were conditioned by intellectual – philosophical and theological – developments. These developments were being articulated by scholars and thinkers, and such articulations registered shifts that were ongoing in their social imaginaries as a whole. The construction of religion as a distinct phenomenon in human life depended on a clear distinction between revelation (or 'grace') and nature, between God and creation, between the self and the world, and between the transcendent ('up there') and the immanent ('down here') (Dupré 1993). In other words, the notion of 'religion' as something discreet

---

[15] Stroumsa is thinking of how religion became an object of ethnology. But thereby, religion also became an object of politics.

was inconceivable without the loss of a sacramental understanding of reality. This sacramental understanding was not necessarily a perfectly coherent or harmonious world view, but it did allow for a symbolic representation of the unity and interweaving of transcendent and immanent realities. A painting like El Greco's 'The Burial of Count Orgaz' (1586), with its strictly horizontal depiction of the separation of heaven and earth – with the priest as the sole meditating figure – brilliantly expresses this new symbolic order that came to the fore in early modern Europe. This horizontal line is repeated on the frontispiece of Thomas Hobbes' *De Cive* (1642/47), where nature and culture (or politics) are strictly kept 'downstairs' and *religio* kept upstairs. In philosophical terms, such a world view depends on a strict determination of the finite-infinite relationship and, eventually, a philosophical determination of the bounds of finitude so that the finite subject or world may be known with exactness and certainty (Milbank 2006, 280).

Such complex intellectual developments in the late Middle Ages and the early modern period all contributed to and registered the arrival of what Charles Taylor calls 'the immanent frame': a standpoint from which the world represents a stable and univocal order, where the self is 'buffered' and disciplined, society is constructed[16], rationality is instrumental, and time secular (Taylor 2007, 542). For modern Europeans, this frame 'constitutes a "natural" order, to be contrasted to a "supernatural" one, an "immanent" world, over against a possible "transcendent" one'.

While Taylor especially focused on intellectual changes, these changes were themselves conditioned by massive institutional and political rearrangements. The Reformation and its settlements, and then the Thirty Years' War, led to a transformation of ecclesial authority, including a secularisation of property and removal of ecclesial jurisdiction (Berman 2003). The modern state expanded through the centralisation of administration, the creation of standing armies, and an enormous increase in taxation.[17] The modern state was increasingly understood in much more abstract terms, and under absolutism, a clearer distinction appeared between 'society' and the 'state' (Skinner 2009; Williams 2014, 291–94).[18] None of these developments, only gestured towards here, do in themselves explain the modern distinction between religion and politics, for our received understanding of these terms came about gradually. It was theorised later by intellectuals, who had some real-world developments in mind. Still, they were essential conditions within which the distinction between

---

[16] As opposed having its origin in a divinely sanctioned natural order.

[17] I do not mean to attribute European state formation entirely to war. Recent scholarship has challenged such 'Bellicist' theories. See Møller and Doucette (2022); Grzymała-Busse (2023).

[18] See also Reinhart Koselleck's famous study (Koselleck 2018).

religion and politics could make sense. Talal Asad contextualises the aforementioned intellectual changes within the growth of the modern state. The state grew and transformed in response to a series of 'problems', including 'the need to control the increasingly mobile poor in city and countryside, to govern mutually hostile Christian sects within a sovereign territory, and to regulate the commercial, military, and colonizing expansion of Europe overseas' (Asad 1999, 185). Within this context, the world is divided into 'a world of self-authenticating things in which we really live as social beings and a religious world that exists only in our imagination' (Asad 1999, 188).

Without many of these enormously complex changes, 'religion' (or 'monotheism') would not be what it is for many today. The notion of religion as we know it requires something like this view of the world to be imaginable – that is, it requires a clear separation between the transcendent and the immanent, and a differentiation between politics and religion. Already in the seventeenth century, intellectuals began to understand that identifying religion as a distinct human phenomenon might have great political significance. If religion could be understood and explained, its political valence could be appreciated or effaced. The distinction between politics and religion inevitably led to differing opinions about religion's political meaning. Was it something so dangerous to political authority that it had to be removed from society altogether? Could it perhaps be privatised and rendered non-political? Or could it indirectly or directly justify or support political authority? These options arose because, when the state has been abstracted from society, pressing questions about how the state is legitimised or challenged began to surface, and religion represented one possible answer.

Thus, after the conflicts and wars of the sixteenth and seventeenth centuries, Enlightenment discourse began to theorise religion both as a source of disorder and a source of legitimacy. In the words of J. G. A. Pocock, it is possible to describe the Enlightenment as 'a family of intellectual and political programs, taking shape in several west European cultures between 1650 and 1700, with the shared but diversified intention of seeing that there be no recurrence of the Wars of Religion' (Pocock 1997, 8). Pocock claims that this context explains why 'enthusiasm' – the sectarian identification of a particular human mind with God, which threatened to create chaos to political order – became the 'antiself' of Enlightenment.

This is part of the context in which the term 'monotheism' was coined. The term came into use in the seventeenth century and is often attributed to the Cambridge Platonist Henry More (1614–87) (More 1660, 62, 188). Yet, there is at least one usage in Latin some years earlier, by the German Benedictine Abbot, David Gregor Corner, who in 1642 wrote that '[j]ust as monarchy is between anarchy and polyarchy, so monotheism is the middle between atheism and polytheism' (Corneri 1642, 303). Corner's typology of different constitutions is ancient, and well-known in classical literature and the church fathers, though the term monotheism is not. More's use of the term was partly inspired by John Selden's pioneering comparative work on Semitic mythology in the *De dis Syris,* published in 1617 (Stoll 2009, 73–77). With Selden's Orientalist work, we find an early example of 'monotheism' being included in a cluster of comparative terms, which would eventually include those of 'atheism', 'polytheism', 'deism', and 'pantheism'. The rise of this series of comparative terms indicates a broader shift towards an understanding of 'religion' as a particular aspect of human life and, eventually, as a *genus* of traditions that express this aspect in different ways.

After Henry More, 'monotheism' was a concern primarily among Enlightenment writers. Daniel Lombard, an English historian, used the term to describe church disputes in the seventh century in his *A Succinct History of Ancient and Modern Persecutions* of 1747, which he wrote as a warning in light of the recent political and religious conflict in his country (Lombard 1747, 60). David Hume (1711–76) famously compared the effects of monotheism, polytheism, and pantheism in *The Natural History of Religion* (1757), which proposed a developmental account of religion (Hume et al. 2008). He noted that polytheism might be more tolerant than monotheism and that polytheism was the original form of religion. He thereby challenged the common view of his day that monotheism was the natural form of religion, as we saw earlier. Hume's comparison of fundamentally different types of religion depended on the idea that religion was a distinct human phenomenon with its particular causes and operations.

The term monotheism, then, arose at a time when religion was being conceptualised, and in which its relationship to politics became a contested issue. In the seventeenth and eighteenth centuries, a number of thinkers sought to deal with the disorderly potential of religion. Thinkers such as Thomas Hobbes (1588–1679), Hugo Grotius, Christian Thomasius (1655–1728), Samuel Pufendorf (1632–1696), or Baruch Spinoza (1632–1677), all sought in different ways to 'position' religious truth within human life in order to restrict its political influence. For Samuel von Pufendorf, both 'Natural and Revealed Religion' demanded that one worships God 'in his own Person', yet precisely as an individual, religious act – not as a civic matter (Pufendorf 2002, 13).

However, the recognition of the Christian Hebraists and some English deists that religion – particularly the belief in the One God – was essential to political life persisted throughout the Enlightenment. Such a faith could be defended rationally and in moral or sociopolitical terms. Jean-Jacques Rousseau's (1712–1778) political philosophy represents one notable attempt to relate religion to society and politics while ensuring it had beneficial political effects. Rousseau understood faith as a natural and deeply felt human need, even if ultimately beyond the realm of knowledge.[19] Rousseau thought that faith might be instrumental to social life and that a public form of worship might even be necessary for political order. However, it was only by strictly defining the legitimate form of religious feeling and pacifying its troubling political consequences that Rousseau would grant its role. Religious *truth* has no positive significance for political life, even if religion has social value.

If a range of thinkers found the idea of a natural monotheistic religion appealing, though many nonetheless worried about the role of religion in political life – what were they actually worried about? In short, they worried about the possibility of revelation, understood as a donation of truth that could not be rationally justified or articulated. This worry was grounded in a strict distinction between the transcendent and the immanent and articulated through a double classification of religion: a 'natural', 'rational', or 'primal' religion on the one hand, and 'positive', 'revealed', or 'historical' religion on the other. For the deists, this distinction echoed the sophist distinction between nature and convention, so that positive religions were placed 'outside the ordered realm of nature and into the category of arbitrary human conventions', or, for some, were equated in entirety with the content of natural religion (Harrison 1990, 7). By contrast, some defenders of Christianity would claim that positive religion adds what natural religion cannot provide (Broughton 1732).

Jan Assmann is interested in this distinction from his perspective as an Egyptologist, for this double sense of religion was understood by some Enlightenment thinkers as characteristic of Egyptian society in particular (Assmann 2014). They thought that Egyptian religion was structured around a distinction between a private, 'esoteric' religion for the elites, and a public, 'exoteric' religion for the people. A distinction between secret and public religion enabled, on the part of Enlightenment deists and atheists, a theory of public religion as a form of 'political theology', that is, as a 'political functionalization of religion'. Whereas an apolitical form of deism or pantheism might be entertained and secretly transmitted by a political-intellectual elite, public and positive religion is there to maintain political order. Esoteric religion must be kept secret precisely because it would be politically dangerous for those in power if the people were disenchanted with the spells of public religion. Thus, for some deists, natural religion is wholly philosophical and must therefore be distinguished from 'civil' theology or religion in Varro's sense, that is, as a popular and mythic (fabulous) form of religion that appeals to the 'lower'

---

[19] Rousseau most clearly expressed his view on religion in the Profession of Faith of the Savoyard Vicar in Émile. See Rousseau (2012, 987–88).

senses of human beings to justify political power. Because the deists denied revelation, Christianity and all revealed religions were considered 'fabulous'; they were deemed fictional political theologies.

Although monotheism, understood as the belief in the One True God, could be deemed as a necessary glue to social life and justification of political rule, Enlightenment thinkers tended to equate 'positive' religion precisely with the Abrahamic traditions since, as religions of the book, they were based on revelation. 'Revealed', 'supernatural', or 'positive' religion came to be identified with Christianity, Judaism, and Islam as organised, ritualised, and institutional realities based on revelation recorded in Scripture, articulated in doctrine, and expressed in practice. It was these religions that some Enlightenment thinkers framed as 'enthusiastic'. 'Throughout the eighteenth century, Deists and pantheists alike sought to escape the yoke of the God of Abraham', Guy Stroumsa writes (Stroumsa 2021, 60–61). In this case, however, the major monotheistic traditions were identified not with the universalism of God's covenant with Abraham in the book of Genesis but with the exclusivism of the Mosaic distinction. This rejection of the Abrahamic traditions is what Stroumsa calls 'the Abrahamic eclipse' in the Enlightenment (Stroumsa 2021, 62).

Election and revelation were deemed dangerous since they disrupted the confines of the immanent frame and prohibited rational explication. In this context, monotheism came to be viewed as potentially absolutistic and antagonistic: A religion of pure revelation, built on an extrinsic donation of truth, cannot mediate its truth with the world; its truth can only be accepted or rejected. Those who seek to occupy the same space as this truth or follow another truth are committing an act of idolatry. Hence, religious truth can motivate political antagonism and disorder if it is not kept strictly separate from those truths that might affect public life. For philosophers like Kant, who followed cues from the deists and Rousseau's understanding of faith, the goal was to mediate between positive and rational religion by reinterpreting and reconstructing established religion in the image of rational religion. Kant claimed there was only one true religion, even if there were many kinds of faith (Kant 1996, 6:12). While he argued that there is no knowledge of religious truth, he thought that the natural regard for the moral law we have as human beings arose from a practical reason whose implications included a rationally necessary faith in God. He thus considered the rational belief in God essential to morality and politics (DiCenso 2011). The true religion was, naturally, monotheistic (Kant 1998, A 590 / B 618). After German Idealism, this question of mediation between 'natural' and 'positive' religion was often repeated by Protestant theologians.

What, then, do these complex religious and political transformations of early modern Europe tell us about the political significance of monotheism? I am suggesting that monotheism became politicised in early modern Europe as a part of wide-ranging disputes about political legitimacy and its relationship to religious authority. 'Religion' became a term of translation that could weaken the Mosaic distinction, as per Reeh, but only because another facet of Christian monotheism had been severely strengthened: the distinction between creator and creature, or the transcendent and the immanent. For this reason, however, the Mosaic distinction was also strengthened, as illustrated by the Enlightenment fear of enthusiasm. When the transcendent and the immanent were understood in competitive terms, any direct incursion of religious truth into political realities risked enhancing competition and antagonism. Within this framework, 'monotheism' could be understood as a particular *kind* of religion with its characteristic political effects – in both universalist and particularist directions. This ambivalence was echoed in the notions of positive and natural religion, which produced a deep split within the theological sources and ideas of the Christian tradition.

The modern debates about the politics of monotheism are thus inextricable from the very idea of religion as it was shaped in early modern Europe. In the eighteenth century, however, yet another taxonomy emerged, as Stroumsa has shown. Developments in linguistics and history led scholars to distinguish between Indo-European and Semitic languages.[20] These developments contributed to a new taxonomy that challenged the old Christian map of religion. Greek and Latin cultures were now associated with the Aryans and the Hebrews with the Semites. With a new taxonomy based on language, Europeans began associating Christianity with the Aryan instead of the Semitic, implying the Indo-European roots of Christian culture and religion. This shift, too, meant that Europeans took an ambivalent stance towards monotheism. This 'ambivalence echoed and amplified those trends in the radical Enlightenment that had grown strongly critical of Christianity beyond the established churches, more broadly of monotheism, and even of the very idea of religion' (Stroumsa 2021, 6). The ambivalence towards monotheism was further complicated since Islam and Judaism were associated with the Near East, and Christianity with Indo-European sources.

Despite these changes, we find that some of the fundamental issues and duplicities inherent to the relationship between monotheism and politics persisted long after the Enlightenment. The concepts of religion devised in the previous centuries were not merely ideas of scholars but also constructions of state apparatuses used by lawyers, politicians, and diplomats and deeply rooted in modern institutions and social structures. With its separation between society and state, the modern state demanded of people and politicians a particular

---

[20] Masuzawa covers some of the same ground in Masuzawa (2005).

epistemic framework for political life within which political issues could be described and resolved in univocal terms (Scott 2020). Only thus could the state gain the right kind of abstraction, and therefore neutrality, vis-à-vis society. Within this framework, religion had to be correctly defined so it could be governed, used, or held at bay.

The relationship between the state and society and its implied epistemological and metaphysical pictures stand at the core of the modern European ambivalence towards monotheism. It is worth mentioning that precisely these constructions of the state's transcendence (including religion) over society justified both defenders and critics of the state in describing it as a kind of 'god' (Nicholls 1989). It is why Hobbes described the Leviathan as a 'Mortal God', and why Karl Marx and Michael Bakunin, in their respective ways, understood the state as a transcendent and authoritarian god-figure (Bakunin 1970; Marx 1994). Within the confines of these analogies, the state's relationship to society – individuals, groups, and mediating institutions – actualises the question of idolatry: whom or what in society can rise to the level at which they become a challenger to the state? At what point does one's allegiance to a certain idea, group, or truth come into conflict with one's responsibility as a citizen?

These analogies – which translate into real political issues – are grounded in a more profound overlap between the social imaginaries of the modern West and those traditions we have come to call monotheistic. The state and its distinction from society, which depends in part on the distinction between politics and religion, echoes the firm difference between transcendent and immanent truth. In this way, the state is a product of a social imaginary that fixes something of real theological contestation in Christianity, Judaism, and Islam. In positioning 'religion' as a human phenomenon that could be neatly defined and separated from political life, it takes a particular 'religious' position.

4 Challenging the Distinction

We can now see how Assmann follows some of the currents of the European Enlightenment I have been pointing to. He seeks to deny our access to 'absolute' truth to make room for a pragmatic approach to politics and a tolerant religion. For Assmann, this change of perspective is demanded by the processes of globalisation, which force religion 'to think beyond its absolute truth-claims and to envisage a common framework within which differences can be recognised and discursively worked through' (Assmann 2014, 156). Today, the distinction between true and false cannot be grounded in revelation, he claims. Instead, 'we must make the Mosaic distinction the object of incessant reflection and redefinition, subjecting it to a "discursive fluidification" (Jürgen Habermas), if it is to remain, for us, the indispensable basis for an advance in humanity' (Assmann 2010, 120).

Assmann's position implies a de-theologised theory of politics and a double theory of religion. It implies a de-theologised theory of politics because it assumes the strict distinction between religion and politics, even if some interaction may be admitted in almost every instance. In fact, Daniel Steinmetz-Jenkins argues that in a certain sense, 'the constructive aspect of Assmann's work presents itself as nothing more than the modern attempt to *de-theologize* the political' (Steinmetz-Jenkins 2011, 527).

One should note that Assmann does not want to denigrate religion as such. He actually points to its potential for peace precisely because it is originally or essentially distinct from politics. Of course, both primary and secondary religions have their ways of both differentiating and fusing religion and politics. Yet, Assmann wants to draw on both senses, while correcting their one-sidedness. From primary religion, he takes the idea that cult and justice must be kept separate. From secondary religion, he takes the idea that absolute truth is strictly different from temporal reality, and thus that it provides a perspective from which to challenge the totalisation of the political:

> Religion can exert its counterpower against the political only if it has recourse to totally different means and values. The truth of this lesson, which is implied in many of Jesus' words and actions, has been demonstrated in modern times by Mahatma Gandhi, who based his nonviolent but extremely powerful actions on the religious idea of 'truth.' It has by now become imperative to dissociate religion from violence. Violence belongs to the sphere of the political, and a religion that uses violence fails to fulfill its proper mission in this world and remains entangled in the sphere of the political. The power of religion rests on nonviolence. Only through a complete rejection of violence is monotheism able to fulfill its liberating mission of forming an alternative counterpower to the totalizing claims of the political.

The sui generis distinction between politics and religion is nonetheless necessary for him to describe the 'counter-religion' of Moses as a 'political religion, in the sense of a sacralized political movement' (Assmann 2005, 148). For Assmann, this is not an admirable feature of monotheism but explains its potential for violence. He laments that 'the Old Testament systematically annuls the distinction, so fundamental to the Egyptian model, between 'cult' and 'justice' – that is, between religion and politics (Assmann 2014, 173). The problem with 'secondary religions' – monotheisms – is that they 'arise from a process of de-differentiation' of politics and religion – that is, cult and justice. Thus, the exclusivism of monotheism is 'originally a political concept' imported into the religious domain, from where it can motivate dangerous political acts (Assmann 2005, 148). At the same time, monotheism also differentiates the absolute and the relative, so that, if only monotheism learns to reject violence, it can relativise the political without propagating religious violence.

While Assmann is operating at a level of both ancient history and cultural memory, I submit that his own categories belong primarily to the latter. Assmann affirms the double theory of religion inherited from the Enlightenment, although as transformed by Moses Mendelssohn (1729–86) and others into a 'religion of mankind'. The theory distinguishes between particular confessions on the one hand and a universal or general religiousness on the other. This theory is part of a new consciousness 'that would prove capable of thinking and feeling beyond the horizon of its quasi-natural 'thick' relations', he maintains (Assmann 2014, 148). He thus imports these ideas from history to the level of contemporary analytical concepts.

Assmann himself utilises Thomas Luckmann's distinction between 'visible' and 'invisible' religion, which represents the difference between the implicit 'universe of meaning' that defines an 'individual's relationship to society and the 'world'', and religion as something 'manifested in specific institutions of the cult and the priesthood' (Assmann 2014, 163). He also employs the theologian Theo Sundermeier's distinction between primary and secondary religions, as noted previously. Sundermeier describes primary 'religious experience, the basis of all piety' as 'directed to vital life' and defined as 'the participation of human beings in their world' (Sundermeier 1997, 392). Secondary religion, by contrast, 'replaces sense intuition by comprehensive rational conceptualization' (Sundermeier 1997, 393). Secondary religion introduces doctrine, demands a decision and inner renewal, conceptualises transcendence, and distinguishes truth from falsehood.

Sundermeier's distinctions and Assmann's use of them reflect a broadly Protestant and Enlightenment understanding of religion, as inherited from the modern European experience. These concepts of primary and secondary religion are themselves part of the legacy of the Reformation, colonial encounters, and the memories of and myths about the Wars of Religion, as we have seen. Insofar as 'secondary religion' signifies the incipient development of modern Western culture, it enforces a sense of Western exceptionality (Winnerman 2021, 173). On the one hand, 'primary' religion reflects the European experience of religion as an 'immediate', pre-rational social glue – it is an inheritance of the 'natural religion' of deist and romantic thought. On the other hand, 'secondary' religion echoes the idea of religion as doctrine contending for truth, something that must be separated from public practice and 'neutralised' with regard to their political effects. It is the realm of 'positive religion'.

When we situate Assmann's conceptual apparatus within the theologico-political history of Europe, we see that Assmann's concepts stem from developments within monotheistic traditions themselves. Assmann is eager to stress that his concern with monotheism is not to do with the question of oneness or mediating figures such as saints or angels but with the distinction between true and false religion, which is the very definition of monotheism (Assmann 2010, 119). However, I believe that the question of the number of gods is relevant, for it touches on the relationship between God as absolute truth and everything else, and thus also the ban on images and the issue of representation.

If we consider the issue of idolatry in epistemological terms, then we can see that Assmann's distinction between absolute and pragmatic truth is precisely part of the inheritance of monotheism in modern European thought. The sharp distinction between true and false religion is only possible when the distinction between the absolute and the relative is secured. Hence, according to Assmann's definition, even the denial of absolute truth is monotheistic: a denial of knowledge about the absolute to the benefit of the pragmatic is only possible if first a border is drawn, beyond which one cannot go. Under such a paradigm, the only actual idolatry is that which takes the relative for something absolute; it is that which confuses empirical experience with unknowable transcendent realities. Even if this distinction is contested, the question of idolatry has been discussed in these terms from Kant to Martin Heidegger or Jacques Derrida (Vries 1999; Benson 2002).

Assmann stands in this post-Enlightenment tradition. At the end of the day, he promotes quite a conventional liberal view: First, religion and politics must be kept separate. Second, religious people can claim allegiance to a particular understanding of the absolute truth, but must recognise a general religiousness, and thus that there is a general relationship to the truth to which nobody can claim ownership. Absolute religious truth-claims are only allowed on the level of institutionalised 'visible religions'. However, if such truth claims, which are grounded in claims to revelation, are taken as universal truths, they become problematic. The most foundational symbolic parameters of a society simply cannot be decided by appeals to revelation, which cannot be reasoned with. Therefore, if an 'invisible' or universal religion is to work in a global age, it must be transformed into a secular discourse of civility. Natural religion must become universalising reason (Assmann 2016, 128–29). Thus, Assmann promotes the same kind of approach to religion as that of many Enlightenment thinkers: By splitting the idea of religion into two, he can argue that confessional religion must be kept outside the domain of political influences, while promoting a non-political concept of general religiousness that is subject to the demands of reason. This latter construction is necessary to temper religious fanatics by imposing on them a reflexive moment of understanding that there are other ways of being religious, yet also necessary to preserve the function of religion as a kind of social glue on local, national, or global levels.

There are several other issues with Assmann's theory of religion and politics. The distinction between primary and secondary religion insinuates that reflective monotheistic theology operates according to a purified and unified logic, whereas religious practice is manifold and complex. However, this is to downplay that theology – the acts of reflective and discursive explication and innovation – itself thematises not only the fluidity of practice but also language and representation as such. Furthermore, Assmann's distinction disregards that practice may also close down issues that thought seeks to hold open. Monotheistic reflection often puts enormous pressure on thought and language (Hart 2013).

For these reasons, Assmann's modern categories for understanding mono-theism skew the meaning of idolatry in Jewish, Christian, and Islamic traditions. The rejection of idolatry is not merely an unequivocal and antagonistic denial of false religion; it does not merely safeguard the divine name against false ones, for it also raises the difficult question of how the divine name itself may be 'said'. God has been thought to be invisible – his dwelling place was the empty space in the temple between the cherubim (Ex 25:17–22). Despite quite a number of stories indicating the contrary in the Old Testament, this funda-mental belief in the invisibility of God has been preserved in the Abrahamic traditions. At the same time, it stands as a presupposition, not in opposition, to theological reflection about how the divine may be represented. The prominent monotheistic traditions have no shortage of sacramental operations or iconic imaginations, and they would hardly make sense without them. As an example, James F. McGrath notes that, in the Greco-Roman period, while Jews could claim their god was incomparable to anything else and were known for their ban on images, they could nonetheless use amulets or interact with other sacred figures (McGrath 2009, 23–37). These features 'were elements *of* Jewish monotheism in this period rather than a departure from it' (McGrath 2009, 98).

Put differently, the Mosaic abolition of the worship of other gods is conjoined with the prohibition against graven images. In Rabbinic terms, to identify *avodah zara* ('alien worship'), we must understand the difference between the 'right worship of the wrong God' and the 'wrong worship of the right God' (Batnitzky 2000, 18). After the Enlightenment, the rejection of graven images can easily be interpreted as an apophatic restriction on knowledge based on an ontological dualism between God and created beings. Yet, throughout the history of monotheistic religions, it has also continued to spur reflection about and reorientation towards how human beings may or may not appropriately respond to and express divine realities in much more complicated ways than such a dualism can account for. Even in the older strands of the Old Testament, the ban on images is heavily qualified, as with the representation of the divine on the Ark or in the Temple. Thus, the prohibition of images raises the question of the difference between true and false representation, as well as their borderland. This borderland represents a liminal zone that the Enlightenment inheritance obscures. Furthermore, the rejection of images should not necessarily be taken as an unequivocal defence of the written word against the sensuous image, as Assmann does. This claim fits poorly with the development of monotheism in the Old Testament, which is not surprising since it is a valid question whether *any* language can remain purely 'textual' as opposed to iconic.[21]

The point I am making is that the ambiguity Assmann is speaking about cannot be resolved with reference to the difference between religious practice on the one hand and textual theology on the other. Monotheistic religions are not merely 'religions of the book' in contrast to ritual, sensuous, or cultic religions (Assmann 2010, 104). Text and language are always already ritualised and symbolised, and while this may be denied in certain parts of these traditions, it is hardly obfuscated in any general or principled way. Analogously, the cataphatic (affirmative) and apophatic (negative) modes of religious language are not merely different styles, approaches, or interpretations but are intertwined in complex ways in monotheistic traditions.

Assmann believes that monotheism divorces the divine from the world so that God 'turns to face the world as a sovereign power' and the human being becomes an 'autonomous – or rather theonomous – individual' (Assmann 2010, 41–42). I submit that this reads more than a *precis* of a late Medieval or early modern Christian imagination than a faithful representation of monotheism throughout history. Hence, we can finally articulate the prejudice of much modern discourse on monotheism and politics: While it is rightly concerned about monotheism's tendency to absolutise truth, and while it continues to reflect on the meaning of this confession to absolute truth, it circumvents the discussion about the relationship between the absolute and the relative, the transcendent and the immanent. In doing so, it brackets the complex negotiation of the relationship between God and creation, that difficult work of representation that is as essential as the distinction between true and false gods.

In modern political life, monotheism plays a particularly ambivalent role because European concepts of politics and religion assume a strict distinction between the transcendent and the immanent, which means that the confession to absolute truth is inevitably rendered as an intolerant demand to take sides. All you can do is accept the truth donated from above that is – precisely because it is

---

[21] See historical remarks in Schaper (2019, 226). For an engagement with Assmann on this topic and a defence of the iconic nature of Christian and monotheist traditions, see Hedley (2016).

transcendent – inexplicable on immanent, horizontal terms. Assmann compares this with Schmitt's concept of the political. Yet, Schmitt's thought echoes a theology that is, in fact, a minority position in the Christian tradition – a position that assumes a strict dichotomy and leaves no mediation between nature and grace (or, in political terms, between society and the state) (Gray 2007). In the next section, we will see examples of critique from a Christian position of precisely this kind of Schmittian monotheism.

As a Christian theologian, I want to press the point that the politics of monotheism concerns not only the Mosaic distinction between true and false worship but also the distinction between the One God and everything else, which includes the question of how God may be represented in creaturely life. Weighty traditions in Judaism, Christianity, and Islam have emphasised that the belief in the oneness of God is not a statement that the set of all gods contains one object.[22] Rather, the oneness of God is an ineffable attribute. God's singular uniqueness prevents God from ever being a member of a set. For precisely that reason, clarifying the nature of God's transcendence is both an imperative and an impossibility: It is imperative because the commandment against idolatry is only legible if one can distinguish God from false imitations of him – which implies that there may be legitimate imitations too. Maimonides, the twelfth-century towering Jewish philosopher who influenced much subsequent reflection on idolatry, argued that idolatry concerns precisely the way we think about God as such (Maimonides 1956). The rejection of false gods cannot make sense without understanding the prohibition against graven images. At the same time, it is impossible to univocally define the relationship between God and created beings because any frame of comparison will inevitably treat God as part of a higher order. Thus, the imperative to confess God as the Truth, as the One God, propels an exploration of how to distinguish the true God from everything else. Various monotheistic traditions follow different trajectories and negotiate the limits of idolatry in different ways. This is, finally, the reason why it is unhelpful to think of monotheism as a univocal belief whose political ramifications can easily be assessed across space and time. Such approaches tend to erase the variegated political modulations of monotheistic traditions. Furthermore, in tension with key monotheistic traditions, they tend to assume that the confession to the One True God takes the form of an unambiguous cognition of the divine.

---

[22] For some examples from classical Islamic theology, see Winter and El-Bizri (2008). Ramon Harvey, in his development of a Māturīdī theology, notes how to Abū Manṣūr al-Māturīdī (853–944) argues that 'having a likeness allows things to fall under the concept of number, whereas having an opposite makes them liable to extinction when the opposite is destroyed. This makes similarity and opposition the basis for plurality, non-existence and contingent form, all of which God transcends in His unicity' (R. Harvey 2021, 74).

If Assmann's theory of the Mosaic distinction is troubled with these issues, how might we instead think of the politics of monotheism? If we challenge the assumption that monotheism configures a relationship to a transcendent truth 'up' there that may only relate competitively to natural truth and to political life, we can approach the issue by looking at specific traditions and contexts – at how the divine is represented and how such practices of representation may affect political life. Assmann's concepts bear the trace, in part, by a history of Christian monotheism that is far more variegated. In the rest of this Element, I want to turn to a discussion of how the politics of monotheism have worked in Christianity and how one might, from a Christian perspective, approach these issues.

In the Christian tradition, the politics of monotheism achieves a distinctive modulation. Christians have traditionally believed that their God is the One True God. In short, they have pledged fidelity to an absolute truth. Like the traditions of Judaism, Christians believe in God's election of a particular people and in revelation: they relate the One God to a particular covenant and a historical donation of truth. It is this combination – a universal God and a particular revelation in history – that has seemed so problematic after the Enlightenment, as it raises the possibility that only one way of living, acting, or holding power may properly represent the divine. This divine authorisation is especially fickle when the sanction stems from a God who demands unconditional assent. On this basis, it becomes imaginable that those who do not partake in the right kind of worship stand in opposition to the community that does.

However, Christianity, as with other traditions, has deep-seated resources that challenge such antagonistic implications. The development of some of the central tenets of Christian dogma in the early Church was inconceivable without clarifying the meaning of God's oneness and how it might or might not be represented in creaturely terms. Thus, the issue of representation is front and centre in Christian reflections on monotheism and its political consequences, as we will see presently. For a monotheistic religion like Christianity, it is naturally the case that the belief in the One True God has legitimated violent or authoritarian political regimes. In fact, the unity of political rule may be viewed as proof that it is divinely sanctioned. In the Christian tradition, the interaction between the Christian faith and the Emperor of the Roman Empire raised this question for the first time. However, in the early Church, Christians also began to speak of God in ways that might challenge the notion of God's oneness. The confession that God is a trinity forced a reconsideration of God's oneness, and the confession that God had become *incarnate* entailed a reflection on the relationship between God and creation. These debates were not merely doctrinal questions about a 'religious' domain of truth but formed and were formed by the

Christian faith's relationship to political power. Hence, the politics of monotheism is at stake in the most central themes of Christian theology.

5 The Trinity as the End of Political Theology?

In modern theology, the political significance of the early development of the Christian doctrine of God became an area of contestation, not least because the modern ambivalence towards monotheism affected the theological debate in significant ways. Yet, it was only in the twentieth century that Christian theologians approached the issue of monotheism and politics in those terms. In the following two sections, I will examine two strands of theological criticisms of monotheism and its politics from the twentieth century to today. Notable modern Christian theologians have launched quite forceful critique of monotheism, not only because of its theological character but also due to its perceived political consequences. Both strands are motivated by what they think are the deleterious political fallout of monotheism.

To take seriously the implication of theology and politics entails a genuine engagement with the political valence of theological representations and, furthermore, an assessment of their validity. Modern Christian criticisms of monotheism illustrate how the Christian tradition has been critical of its relationship to political power, even as it continues to be deeply entangled with such power. Put differently, they exemplify essential discussions about the meaning and politics of idolatry in the Christian tradition. Nevertheless, I shall argue that these Christian critics of monotheism repeat or echo the Enlightenment contention that monotheistic religion must be separated from political affairs. Although they approach the matter in different ways, they all seek to demarcate monotheism and blame the harmful political consequences of Christianity on that doctrine.

In this section, then, I will discuss the first strand, which runs from the German Church historian Erik Peterson through Jürgen Moltmann, Leonardo Boff, and others. This strand of criticism was reacting in part to the totalitarian regimes of the twentieth century.[23] It understood monotheism as implicit in totalitarianism and found a remedy in the Christian doctrine of the Trinity. This criticism raises the question of to what extent God's unity can be represented in creaturely political life. In the next section, I will turn to another strand, exemplified by Laurel Schneider, which focuses on the doctrine of the incarnation.

The German Church Historian Erik Peterson stands at the beginning of a line of theologico-political critiques of monotheism in the past century. His essay 'Monotheism as a Political Problem: A Contribution to the History of Political Theology in the Roman Empire' was a historical reflection loaded with

---

[23] I will not discuss Boff's critique of 'strict' monotheism in this Element. See Boff (1988, 2000).

contemporary significance (Peterson 2011). Peterson wrote the essay during the Third Reich. The essay was part of his rejection of the kind of 'Reich' theology that would legitimate authoritarian rule, and he particularly had Carl Schmitt's political theology in mind.

Peterson claimed that monotheism as a political problem 'originated in the Hellenistic transformation of the Jewish faith in God' (Peterson 2011, 104). He looked to the Aristotelian doctrine of the highest principle as a self-contemplating mind to understand the introduction of monotheism into Jewish and Christian theologies – monotheism here being understood as *monarchia* ('one ruler'). Although Aristotle did not use the term in this sense, Peterson believed the former contributed to the idea of God as the one monarch and the concern that earthly kings could imitate God's monarchy: 'in the divine monarchy, the single rule (*mia archē*) of the ultimate single *principle* coincides with the actual hegemony of the single ultimate possessor of this rule (*archōn*)' (Peterson 2011, 69).

Peterson also pointed to the old Great King of the first Persian Empire, who mirrors God himself. As with God, the king ruled over all with perfect power (*dynamis*) yet was at a distance from the concrete operations of everyday life (Peterson 2011, 70). This theologico-political construction was also available to the Jewish philosopher Philo of Alexandria (20 BCE–50 CE), who used the Peripatetic ideas of monarchy. However, Peterson claims that Philo's Jewish doctrine of creation made him reject an emanationist ontology that would allow God's power to be mediated in creaturely terms, thus ruling out the possibility of venerating worldly rulers (Peterson 2011, 72–75). Instead, he used it as a 'politico-theological concept' in a different way; he sought to defend God's monarchy in order 'to justify the superiority of the Jewish people and their mission to paganism' (Peterson 2011, 78).

Peterson notes that the word 'monarchy' was widely used among early Christian theologians, including the apologist Justin Martyr (100–165). Again, borrowing from Jewish writers and traditions, it is used to justify the superiority of God's people (Peterson 2011, 78). It was only with Tertullian (155–220) and debates about what would become the doctrine of the Trinity that the term became controversial, Peterson claims (Peterson 2011, 81). Praxeas the grammarian (second/third century) had used the idea of God's 'monarchy' to argue that the Father and the Son had to be identical since true rule cannot be divided. For his part, Tertullian responded that it is perfectly possible for a monarch to share his rule with a son (Peterson 2011, 81–82). Peterson claims that Tertullian's argument follows the same logic as defenders of polytheism, who saw no contradiction between a heavenly monarch and a multitude of lesser gods or powers.

In Origen of Alexandria (185–254) and his followers, which included Eusebius of Caesarea (260/5–339), Peterson finds another problematic use of the idea of God's monarchy. The second-century Greek philosopher Celsus characterised Christian monotheism as a form of revolt, that is, the attempt by one group to upset the hierarchy and unity in the Roman Empire. Celsus thought it impossible for all people to believe in one God, which is why one needed a polytheism in which many gods ruled in the hearts of different peoples, while a transcendent God reigned over all. Origen's response was to point to the eschatological hope that God would one day be the ruler of all peoples, thus proving that Christianity was more than a sectarian movement. Origen saw the *Pax Augusta*, the two-centuries-long Roman peace, as a sign of that impending rule. In that way, Christian monotheism was turned into a legitimating ideology for the Roman Empire: 'There should be no mistake that the whole conception linking empire, peace, monotheism, and monarchy consists of a unity fashioned by Christians,' Peterson wrote (Peterson 2011, 96). The Arians followed this line of thinking, turning monotheism into 'a political imperative, a *Reichspolitik*'.

However, precisely because of this theologico-political function of monotheism, the doctrine of the Trinity 'threatened the political theology of the Roman Empire' (Peterson 2011, 103). When, finally, the Cappadocian Fathers (Basil the Great, Gregory of Nyssa, and Gregory of Nazianzus) formulated the orthodox doctrine of the Trinity, this connection between the Christian belief in God and the Empire was severed, according to Peterson. Monarchical political theology was 'bound to founder on the trinitarian dogma' (Peterson 2011, 104). Gregory of Nazianzus (329–390) claimed that the monarchy of the Triune God was a unity that 'had no correspondence in the created order', according to Peterson (Peterson 2011, 103). The Trinity was unrepeatable and unrepresentable. 'With such arguments', Peterson claimed, 'monotheism is laid to rest as a political problem', and the 'linkage of Christian proclamation to the Roman Empire was *theologically* dissolved'. Even more, the doctrine of the Trinity 'resolved' monotheism as a political problem in general and made a 'fundamental break' with 'every "political theology" that misuses the Christian proclamation for the justification of a political situation' (Peterson 2011, 104). Whereas the doctrine of the Trinity resolved the issue in the East, St Augustine's eschatology played a similar role in the West by claiming that no ruler could present himself as definitively aligned with the will of God before the end of history.

Peterson's argument has been fiercely discussed and criticised ever since (Schindler 1978; Geffré, Jossua, and Lefébure 1985). Scholars have noted several problems with his short but dense essay. Some of these issues concern historical accuracy. Peterson is wrong, for example, to claim that the notion of divine monarchy derives solely from Peripatetic sources; there are clear traces, such as in Psalm 82, of the notion of God as 'single figure surrounded by minor powers' – an idea that simplifies earlier polytheistic Pantheons (Smith 2003, 47). Furthermore, as James W. Haring points out, Judaism employed a pattern common to Near Eastern ideas of kingship, where the human monarch is adopted or derived from the divine monarchy (Haring 2017, 519). In fact, it was only during Israel's experience of exile, when a political theology of this sort seemed impossible, that there arose a sense that Yahweh's kingship was incomparable (Haring 2017, 521). Haring, however, notes that the expansion of Yahweh's rule to the world as a whole does not necessarily entail the impossibility of every theologico-political analogy. Indeed, the analogy Peterson is most concerned about is between God and the emperor – an analogy grounded in precisely the universalism of Yahweh's rule. As Assmann notes, so 'little monotheism suits the needs of a national religion, so well it functions as an imperial religion' (Assmann 2005, 150). Furthermore, his claim that the Cappadocians left behind the idea of God's monarchy is flat-out wrong since they explicitly affirm God's monarchy (Mrówczyński-Van Allen 2017, 580).

Peterson fails to establish his claim that monotheism is the ground of political theology in general, both because monotheism is more essential to the traditions that he seeks to recover and because his dogmatic alternative – the doctrine of the Trinity – has been used to legitimate imperial power as well. In fact, Eusebius interpreted Constantine's three successors as imitating the Trinity (Ruggieri 1985, 18). Ottmar John notes that even if the doctrine of Christ's divinity or the Trinity challenges an ideological use of faith, it does not follow that one can make the general deduction, '[w]here there is dominion, there is no belief in the Triune God' (John 1996, 60). The doctrine of the Trinity and Christ's divinity only challenge ideological uses of faith within their concrete stories of God's revelation to the oppressed people of Israel. Thus, Jürgen Manemann argues that monotheism can only be instrumentalised when separated from the story of Exodus, which contextualises monotheism as a message of hope for the oppressed (Manemann 2002, 338). Such claims are debatable, but they build on the sound insight that monotheism's political function depends on the matrix of narratives, symbols, and ideas it is expressed through, as well as the pragmatic setting it operates within.

There are other questions about Peterson's argument as well. As mentioned, Peterson wrote his essay in the tense theologico-political situation of Nazi Germany. Carl Schmitt raised the question of political theology in his book *Political Theology: Four Chapters on Sovereignty* during the early years of the Weimar Republic and wrote a bitter response to Peterson much later (Schmitt 2005, 2008). Schmitt rightly points to the significance of the religious and political situation in which Peterson wrote his essay. In Peterson's time, the distinctions between the religious and the political were in flux because the established institutions of Church and State had been dislodged (Schmitt 2008, 43–44). In such a context, Schmitt claims, everything becomes potentially political, yet everything has also become potentially a theological question.

Viewed in this light, Peterson's concern about the theologico-political uses of monotheism can be seen as part of an attempt to re-establish the separation between religion and politics by means of a dogmatic definition. Schmitt's pointed question – which nonetheless springs out of a dangerous political position – is whether a dogmatic exclusion of monotheism is viable without a dogmatic *authority*. And if one admits the necessity of authority, does it make sense to say one is dealing with something beyond the political? Even if one assumes the importance of ecclesial authority (the magisterium, the episcopate, or ecumenical councils) for theological reflection, a trans-historical verdict about the *impossibility* of a Christian political theology based on monotheism seems far from plausible. Impossibility is a feature of necessity; it arises only when there is no ambivalence about authority. What Schmitt understood was that the distinction between the temporal and the spiritual, or the immanent and the transcendent, cannot be universally assumed; it is only delineated by certain ideas and practices rooted in forms of life. Thus, neither an epistemological closure in a Kantian sense nor a dogmatic closure is a really viable option.

The theological point is that to decidedly exclude the very *possibility* that monotheism might be Christian and that such a monotheism might legitimate authoritarian or problematic political regimes is to abstract faith and dogma from the vicissitudes and atrocity of history. Dogma is never politically innocent; it is enmeshed in the ambivalence of human authority. Furthermore, Peterson's attempt to shield dogma from the politics of authority leaves the Church with the task of 'abandoning' earthly rule to the detriment of its witness in political life. In this way, it may contribute to unduly secularising political space while leaving it open to other religious and non-religious claims to authority (Mrówczyński-Van Allen 2017, 573). It leaves the Church resource-less to evaluate and differentiate between theological conceptions at play in the political sphere. For this reason, Artur Mrówczyński-Van Allen claims – admittedly perhaps a bit too sharply – that Peterson's attempt to avoid totalitarianism might 'help pave the way' for it (Mrówczyński-Van Allen 2017, 581).

However, if no politics is theologically innocent, we can also be decidedly critical of Carl Schmitt's understanding of political theology. To open the question of political theology is also to open the question of theology, and theology is undermined when it is reduced to the machinations of power. The problem is not necessarily monotheism as such, but a theology that conceives of a God as a fount of arbitrary and unrestricted power, a theology inherited from late Medieval nominalism and shaped by the modern immanent frame that resists both horizontal and vertical mediation (Mrówczyński-Van Allen 2017, 580). By contrast, I venture that theology cannot be reduced to brute decisions or irrational assents to a higher truth: it allows for conversion and conversation, it is moved by the insights gained in inexpressible depths of interiority and the raptures of glory, yet also by the authority of argument. Most Christian traditions assume that there is a public character to theology that cannot be reduced to individual experience or the ideologies of established authorities. If theological discourse matters, it must have at least some integrity; we cannot, in other words, be entirely and constantly misled about what determines the discourse (Williams 1991). That is why I believe Peterson was right in looking at the role of monotheism in the Christian tradition, even if he was wrong in claiming that the linkage between the Christian God and imperialism had been settled once and for all. Theology matters, even if it offers no guarantee against abuse or unintended consequences.

Peterson's thesis about the closure of Christian political theology inspired theologians after the Second World War, even if its legacy was used for another kind of opening of political theology. Most notably, the German theologian Jürgen Moltmann built on Peterson's critique of monarchical political theologies. Commenting on the theology of the Christian Roman Empire, he claimed: 'The legitimation model for the Christian emperors was the correspondence to the divine-world monarchy: one God, one Christ, one emperor, one religion, one empire' (Moltmann 1986, 49). There is an interesting genealogical claim in the prefatory note in Peterson's essay, namely that the 'European Enlightenment preserved nothing of the Christian belief in God except "monotheism", implying a reduction and loss of a richer theological vision in some ways preserved until then' (Peterson 2011, 68). There is a good reason to assume that Peterson is thinking of Enlightenment deism, although he says nothing more about this narrative of decline, which qualifies his whole essay. According to Moltmann, however, the problem of Christian political monotheism lasted *until* the Enlightenment, being 'accepted theological doctrine of sovereignty until the time of European absolutism' (Moltmann 1986, 49). Unfortunately, monotheism is a theological perversion, Moltmann claims. He notes that even someone like Genghis Kahn could make use of it in his message to the pope in 1254: 'In heaven there is no other than the one, eternal God; on earth there is no other than the single lord, Genghis Khan, the Son of God' (Moltmann 1986, 49). Monotheism is, in other words, a universal imperialist theology that has nothing specifically Christian about it.

Moltmann claims that the numerical unity of God legitimates an autocratic view of political power. Against monotheism, he summons a theology of the cross – a theology founded on Christ's renunciation of authoritarian power – which entails 'the critical dissolution of self-justification and political foe images, integrations, and oppressions which are produced by political religions' (Moltmann 1986, 53). Furthermore, following Peterson in approach though not in content, he marshals the doctrine of the Trinity against the monarchical model of God. The Father of Jesus is not a monarchical autocrat, but precisely the Father of the crucified Christ; the One who gives his life for others, the One who is victorious in his renunciation of power. For Moltmann, the early Christian disputes reveal that monotheism is incompatible with a full doctrine of Christ's divinity – as illustrated in the heresies of Arianism, which subordinates the Son to the monarchical God, or Sabellianism, which reduces the persons of the Trinity to modes of appearance (Moltmann 1993, 129–37). Moltmann credits Tertullian for developing a robust doctrine of the Trinity that challenges strict Monarchianism yet claims that the latter is unable to avoid the sense that the Son and the Spirit, and thus plurality, are secondary and primarily tied to God's economy (God's history with and workings in creation), not his eternal being. This lapse into abstract oneness is repeated in modern theology – for example, in the theologies of Karl Barth and Karl Rahner – which is bound by the fancies of the bourgeois subject (Moltmann 1993, 139–48). For Moltmann, 'European absolutism of the Enlightenment period was the final form of political monotheism in its religiously legitimated form. It was also the last attempt to establish a state based on religious unity' (Moltmann 1993, 196). In the twentieth century, in the wake of the democratic revolutions, monotheism's secularised legacy is found in conservatism, fascism, and anti-democratic ideologies (Moltmann 1993, 196–97).

Although we have seen historical reasons to challenge the necessary linkage between monotheism and Christian imperialism or absolutism, it is worthwhile to reflect on Moltmann's alternative to monotheism. Moltmann himself wants to secure the unity of God neither through a doctrine of the one substance nor of the one subject, but the 'unitedness' of the three Persons, more specifically, their mutual indwelling (*perichoresis*) – drawing on the now-famous theological term from the Syrian Church Father John of Damascus (675/6–749) (Moltmann 1993, 150). For Moltmann, however, the dead-end of political monotheism can only be 'overcome' by ridding ourselves of 'a universal monarchy of the one God' (Moltmann 1993, 197). Instead, following the idea of *perichoresis*, an authentic doctrine of the Trinity corresponds to,

> a community in which people are defined through their relations with one another and in their significance for one another, not in opposition to one another, in terms of power and possession. (Moltmann 1993, 198)

Thus, Moltmann contributed to launching the project of 'Social Trinitarianism', which opposed the impoverished monotheism of the West with an Eastern Trinitarianism that begins with a multiplicity always already in unity.

Moltmann does not heed Peterson's warning against establishing analogies between God and political life. Whereas Peterson refers both to the Cappadocians' doctrine of the Trinity and Augustine's stress on the eschatological horizon of history as prohibitions against political theology, Moltmann rejects one theologico-political analogy in favour of another. Where Peterson's argument is apophatic – God's inner life is incomparable and unrepeatable in created time – Moltmann's is programmatic: we must reject ruthless monotheism and opt for a theology that motivates a variant of social personalism. Our politics should mirror the Trinitarian coincidence of infinite and incomprehensible individual interiority with total transparency to and indwelling with the other.

In one of the most famous criticisms of Social Trinitarianism, Karen Kilby has argued that it unwittingly lapses into ideology. Social Trinitarianism, Kilby believes, is in danger of projecting 'society's latest ideals of how human beings should live in community' onto God and then claiming that this view of divinity should motivate our own political orientation (Kilby 2000, 441). In line with Ludwig Feuerbach's famous criticism of religion, theology is exposed as an ideology when it is shown to produce a circle of human projections. Kilby's argument is significant and builds on a sense of the limits of human understanding. The difficulty with turning the Trinity into a social ideal is not only that divine reality itself is inscrutable, so our concepts about it must be appropriately qualified, but also that political life is a highly fluid and imperfect reality. Any abstraction of a social ideal from the Trinity must guard against forcefully imposing itself on human social life. Ultimately, Kilby is invoking the danger of *idolatry*, of the possibility that we become 'so confident that we know what we are talking about when we talk about the Trinity, that we are projecting our most pleasing ideas onto God and making those the object of our worship' (Kilby 2010, 66).

Kilby's critique of Social Trinitarianism shifts the focus to the limits and reach of representation, particularly how Christians have come to represent the divine life based on the stories and confessions about God's actions and presence in and as Jesus Christ. The issue is not just how one should think about God's unity but how the Christian belief in Jesus Christ fundamentally shapes the representation of that unity. Kilby is raising the question of idolatry not to exclude political opponents but actually to do the opposite: she is worried that the Christian belief in Jesus Christ is turned into a justification for a particular kind of political programme, as if Christians have some exclusive access to political solutions than others do not. In this way, she is reminiscent of Assmann, who too seeks to deny access to absolute truth, although Kilby's argument is more grounded in a theological consideration than in a post-Enlightenment epistemology. There are important nuances to discuss regarding Kilby's criticism of Social Trinitarianism, but for our purposes, she points to what I take to be the crucial issue in how Christianity may negotiate the relationship between divine truth and political life (Coakley 2021; Kilby 2021; Prevot 2021; Williams 2021).

The issue of representation is a key issue for the politics of monotheism, as I have suggested. If a kind of political claim is made on behalf of a transcendent God, it may seem to demand unconditional surrender to its agenda. Furthermore, if that claim is based not on the discoveries of universal reason or readily available experience but on a particular way of representing God as expressed in a faith based on very specific events in history, it seems to rule out any shared ground on which compromise may be found, or negotiation may occur. This is, at any rate, the worry we have inherited from the Enlightenment. Therefore, we must attend to the role of Jesus Christ, and the incarnation in particular, to interrogate Christian logics of representation.

6 Incarnation and Representation

Peterson shared a similar worry to that of Kilby: If we employ our representations of the divine to sanction a certain vision of political life or to legitimate an unchallengeable political ruler, dangerous consequences may follow. Yet, we cannot represent or imitate the divine in that way, simply because God's unity, as well as God's Trinity, is ontologically different from our created unities and multiplicities, Peterson thought. His rejection of monotheism depended on his understanding of the doctrine of the Trinity and his conviction that the eschatology developed in Western theology structurally prevented any re-enactment of divine life herein. Peterson refers to Augustine's claim that there is no divine action between the ascension of Jesus Christ and His return that can be decidedly verified by human observers (Markus 1988). No political ruler can claim to be the definitive representation of the divine in that period. For that reason, Augustine decidedly rejected a Christian triumphalism that would interpret the *Pax Augusta* as a sign of divine providence.

Nonetheless, Peterson omitted a discussion of the incarnation in his essay on monotheism, which stood at the heart of the Trinitarian debates he was retracing and interwoven with Christian stances towards worldly rule. It is not without reason that Moltmann seeks to develop a political vision out of Christian depictions of Christ's life and work. On this particular issue, he aligns with quite traditional political theologies, including after Constantine.

Moltmann glosses over the fact that the providential and imperialist theology of the Roman Emperor did not merely originate in a reflection on God's monarchy; it was equally motivated by the belief that God had decidedly and victoriously acted in and through Jesus Christ (Demacopoulos 2017, 120).

Even Eusebius, one of the culprits in Peterson and Moltmann's accounts, argued that 'the delusion of the polytheistic error' was resolved only by the divine *logos* taking flesh.[24] Indeed, he believed that *Pax Augusta* was a sign of the providential preparation for nothing other than the incarnation and the Gospel (Oakley 2006, 73). Long after Constantine, dominant traditions of Christian political theology have been as Christological as they have been monotheistic. When the Reformer Martin Luther argued, in his address to the Christian nobility of the German Nation, that Christ 'does not have two different bodies, one temporal and one spiritual' since there is only 'one Head and one body', he challenged the independence of ecclesial jurisdiction, all the while repeating a common dictum in Christian political theology (Luther 1966, 130). Even if, as Augustine believed, there is no way to know that God directly willed *this* particular political ruler, the Christian belief that God's will has been revealed in Jesus Christ may indeed have political consequences; it may inspire specific ways of acting, certain assumptions about what constitutes legitimate political rule, and it may – Assmann warns – lead us to define who our political (and religious) enemies are. Therefore, we must ask how the incarnation may shape Christian views of representation and idolatry.

Early Christian thought not only affirmed the oneness of God but also the importance of a covenant, of an election of God's people who would somehow represent God's Kingdom on earth by being the 'Body of Christ'. This very covenant, they thought, was constituted by God's decisive and revealing act in Jesus Christ. In this way, early Christianity 'drew a line', although not always in the ways that accorded with Jan Assmann's understanding of the Mosaic distinction. Early Christianity justified its reinterpretation of the prohibition against images by identifying Jesus Christ as the 'image of the invisible God' (Col 1:15) (Besançon 2000, 84). This claim was thought of as a modulation, not a denial, of the claim that nobody has seen God (Joh 1:18; 1 Tim 6:16).[25] The idea that Jesus Christ was the definitive revelation of the Father – grounded, for example, in the intimate language of union in John's gospel – reshaped and challenged other Jewish and Hellenic ideas about the divine, but it also sanctioned new representations of God (Hurtado 2005). Philo, the Alexandrian Jewish thinker, spoke of the Word (*logos*) as the image of God, but not as Godself, which is what Christians did (Besançon 2000, 82–84). The Christian doctrine of the Trinity is unimaginable without the incarnation, out of which it historically grew. The claim that Jesus was truly human and truly divine forced a reconsideration of the meaning of idolatry, of what amounted to true and false

---

[24] Cited in Oakley (2006, 73).
[25] Ian A. MacFarland has forcefully argued that Chalcedonian Christology was precisely meant to affirm the invisibility of God. See McFarland (2019).

worship. It shaped Christian understandings of what or who was the elected community (Bauckham 1981; Hurtado 2005). If there is a sanctioned representation of the One True God in Christianity, it is most appropriately traced back to its narratives about Jesus Christ – narratives that could, in themselves, be understood as idolatrous by some. The faith in Jesus Christ strongly implied not only that human signs and actions are capable of representing God in some fashion but that God could even be embodied and ultimately expressed in this symbolic and material world.

This very brief outline does not specify a particular kind of Christian theology, as much as it points to the presupposed background for a multitude of Christian theologies throughout history. For our purposes, however, the key point is that such beliefs about Jesus Christ introduced a new logic of representation into monotheism, with enormous political consequences. Now, it was the life and work of Christ that shaped what a true representation of God might look like. Christian monotheism is, first and foremost, a monotheism shaped by faith in Christ.

Oliver O'Donovan's political theology helpfully spells out this logic of representation implicit in the Christian faith in Christ. According to O'Donovan, Christ is both a mediator of divine rule – thus fulfilling the role of the Davidic monarch – and a representative – the suffering individual of the people (O'Donovan 2005, 123). As a mediator of divine rule, the 'divine authority is irreplaceably immediate in the dying, rising and future disclosing of Jesus' (O'Donovan 2005, 124). As a representative, Jesus Christ constitutes and truly is the presence of the people of God – He is the Body of Christ (O'Donovan 2005, 125). From such short yet packed theses, a range of political conclusions may follow. Yet, the overall point is that a particular kind of mediation of the divine constitutes a new subject – the people of God, Christ's 'Body' – who can properly and rightly live in response to divine activity.

It is precisely this sort of logic that has critics like Assmann worried. Even more, this kind of Christological monotheism has received criticism from theological quarters. The most forceful theological critique from a Christian perspective after Peterson and Moltmann has been that of Laurel C. Schneider in her book *Beyond Monotheism: A Theology of Multiplicity* (2007) (Schneider 2008). Schneider seeks to challenge monotheism *tout court*, and – reversing a long history of Christian reflection – actually refers to incarnation as a fundamental challenge to monotheism, its logic of representation, and its political fallout.[26] Unlike the twentieth-century critics of monotheism, Schneider does not primarily tie monotheism to the authoritarian sovereign

---

[26] I omit the definitive article when discussing Schneider's view of incarnation, since her theology relativises the uniqueness of Christ's incarnation.

state. Instead, she seeks to develop a theological response to a transnational political world: an entanglement of globalised capital, cross-regional wars, and ever-transforming empires:

> [T]his theology emerges out of a specific time and place of political uncertainty, prolonged wars with unclear rationales, and global shifts in power. Guerilla attacks by 'terrorists' and massive, devastating retribution by wealthy 'nations' are impossible to unravel in traditional terms of border disputes, royal lines of succession, or access to industrial wealth. The economics *and* emerging sociology of globalized capital are less and less tied to the idea of 'nations,' meaning that both war and peace conceived in national terms are less coherent and less effective. And theology is as mixed up in politics and the effects of global economics today as it ever has been in history. This is particularly evident in the United States and in the countries of the Middle East, all of which are intimately bound together in struggles for power that, as often as not, are framed in the languages of religious ideologies of monotheism. Theology, particularly theology emerging out of the United States, cannot avoid these struggles over the One God because it is implicated in and made complicit by the effects of American actions on the world and on ourselves. (Schneider 2008, 2)

Schneider wrote her book in a post-9/11 world, though roughly a decade before Donald Trump, Covid-19, or the war in Ukraine – which might explain the debatable post-nationalist framing. Despite what she views as the declining importance of the nation-state, she believes a critique of monotheism is no less relevant in a globalised world. In fact, monotheism is the chief culprit in Schneiders' theologico-political narrative – a narrative of vast historical and political scale. Prefigured in the reign of Akhenaten, a 'logic of the One' has spread throughout the world from the 'context of empire in post-exilic Israel, imperial Greece, and imperial Rome', she maintains (Schneider 2008, 26). This logic is deeper than any ideological expression, it is more of a deep-seated cultural logic, and monotheism is 'the ideological – aspect of a larger cultural framework' (Schneider 2008, 26). Monotheism is the religious articulation of the logic of the One. Schneider is aware of the modern origins of the term monotheism, the ancient historical and religious origins of its theology, and its contemporary significance. However, by understanding monotheism as the ideological aspect of 'the logic of the One' – a term in part inspired by Luce Irigaray – she ties it to a logico-cultural dynamic towards totality and closed identity that seems to be all but universal in its reach.

The theological shape of monotheism is defined by its concept of oneness, Schneider claims. She believes monotheism is unhelpful as a constructive theological term, yet as a 'shorthand' for the logic of the One, the term still has some use. Understood as a kind of logic, we can trace its theological expression in the history of monotheistic religions. Recounting a common narrative, Schneider thinks that monotheism arose in Israel's exilic context as part of a construction of Israelite identity in a difficult political situation. The lack of kingdom, power, and land in exile was fertile soil for an ideology of a victorious divinity and a denial of the existence of all other gods (Schneider 2008, 31–33).

Beyond these humble origins, however, monotheism is 'deployed' by rulers who have searched for 'a divine mirror for their totalitarian dreams of state or of church power' (Schneider 2008, 4). In other words – and the conceptual shifts here are difficult to track – 'Christian monotheism is empire theology' (Schneider 2008, 4). Empire is, for Schneider, understood as 'a shorthand not only for globalised consolidations of power in the hands of the few but also for the logic of the One writ large' (Schneider 2008, 5). The logic of the one is related to 'racism', 'sexism', 'classism', 'heterosexism', 'colonialism', 'ethnocentrism', and 'nationalism' (Schneider 2008, 3). Its contrary is the 'gospel', a 'mobile and always contextualized message of good news to the poor and disenfranchised' (Schneider 2008, 5).

Multiplicity, as intimated in the incarnation, is Schneider's alternative to the logic of the One. Given the discussions earlier, this theological decision is surprising. The doctrine of the incarnation played a significant role in the 'empire theology' of the early Church, as well as in the later ages. Furthermore, it is precisely the incarnation that has been the most derided by post-Enlightenment attacks on Christian monotheism: in Christian theology, the incarnation is the supreme place of revelation, and thus, for what thinkers of the Enlightenment called positivity. The incarnation mediates God's absolute truth in a particular historical instance, thus demanding 'a unique social form of acknowledging him', in the words of Christian Duquoc (Duquoc 1985, 60). The incarnation seems to introduce the Mosaic distinction into the immanent domain if we follow Jan Assmann's terms.

Schneider, however, rejects most traditional interpretations of the incarnation from the early Church to the twentieth century, which she believes has been dominated by the logic of the One, beginning with attempts to fuse it with Hellenistic of divine impassibility and a dichotomy between divine spirit and worldly body (Schneider 2008, 139).[27] Schneider wants to widen the idea of incarnation, to challenge the uniqueness of its location in Jesus Christ, in order to speak of multiple incarnations in the multiplicity of all kinds of bodies.

---

[27] For a critical response to this claim about early Christian theology and its doctrine of creation, see Soskice (2017).

For Schneider, incarnation is a figure for the limits of representation as such. Jesus' body is an iconoclastic figure, and the Mosaic rejection of graven images is ultimately grounded in the body's multiplicity its resistance to abstraction. If 'we wish to say that God *is Love*, then we also say that God comes into being specifically, without abstraction' (Schneider 2008, 206). In her exposition of the singularity of Jesus, she claims that the orthodox interpretations of the incarnation as formulated in the Church councils of Nicaea and Chalcedon effaced Jesus' singular body and reduced his humanity to its commonality with all of humanity. In other words, the Christian logic of representation effaced his particularity. The Church councils 'spoke over his silence' – the silence of Jesus' body, which is most evident in its silence before the imperial and political authorities (cf. Luke 23). In this way, Schneider's theology renders the Word of God 'silent': it 'occurs' but does not speak (Schneider 2008, 175). It is a post-representational transformation of the Christian faith in Jesus Christ.

While Schneider rejects what she thinks of as a Hellenistic dualism and denigration of the body, her prioritising of the body as a locus of multiplicity reiterates an opposition between bodies and 'doctrines', 'ideas', 'abstractions', 'universals', and so forth. 'The challenge of thinking multiplicity is therefore, in part, one of thinking bodies against abstraction, against universals and generalizations' (Schneider 2008, 142). Thus, her defence of incarnation does not involve the mediation of the divine in the worldly but the all-pervasive resistance of bodies to being reduced to the logics of representation or abstraction that constantly face them. Idolatry is now reinterpreted to mean the idolatry of representation as such: 'everything we think or say, teach or proclaim, believe or catechize, is not God, not the Deep, not multiplicity, not enough' (Schneider 2008, 153).

This is not the place to thoroughly consider Schneider's theological project. I will focus on her critique of monotheism before I make some remarks about her view of the incarnation as it pertains to the issue of representation. Schneider's critique of monotheism is helpful in pointing out the tendency within Christian (and other) traditions towards a dominating logic that submits everything to a numerical unity. It is attentive to the fact that there are real correspondences between theological logics of oneness and oppressive political regimes – and that this correspondence is not only related to circumscribed nation-states or individual leaders but fluid international ideologies and self-reproducing logics. However, her argument for why monotheism should be identified with the 'ideological' component of this logic of the One depends on a story so far-reaching, so lacking in integration between overarching narrative and historical detail, that it is hard even to falsify. It evidences a clear case of what I, in other writings, have diagnosed as an overreach in recent theological genealogies (Bergem 2017, 2023).

A deeper issue, however, is at the level of theory and relates to what she calls the logic of the One. Schneider frames the problem of monotheism in a subtle and intriguing way, though in a way that tends towards a questionable reading of history. Schneider admits that history 'is never simple' or 'uniform', and that 'the logic of the One has served both to shore up imperial aspirations to power and, at times, to stand in judgement of those aspirations', yet insists that the history of the 'religions of the One God suggest the very critique that this study undertakes' (Schneider 2008, 4). This admission to complexity is theoretically grounded in her claim that the logic of the One 'is simply *not* One. There is always less, and more, to the story' (Schneider 2008, 1). Furthermore, Schneider does not forgo unity, only the dominance of the One over the Many and its implied duality between unity and plurality.

By framing the issue this way, she nonetheless gives licence to an imposition of a Deleuzian ontology onto history where violence is read as directly resulting from the logic of the One.[28] At the same time, by arguing that the logic of the One is never one, she interprets the presence of elements that escape monotheistic totalities as an unwitting transgression of a pervasive suppressive tendency. But this is the crux of the issue: how do we know that these exceptions in the monotheistic traditions really are suppressed or unwitting exceptions? If there are leakages of multiplicity everywhere, why believe that there was always an intention to prevent leakages? We find, in other words, a similar issue of abstraction to that we saw with Assmann's notion of monotheism.

Citing Ruggieri, Schneider claims that monotheism expresses 'self-interest with a justificatory veneer' (Schneider 2008, 26). This is a hermeneutics of suspicion more often grounded, I submit, not in the plausible interpretation of concrete human intentions but in the posited 'intentions' produced by a highly specific ontological construction. In other words, I worry that her genealogical endeavour feeds on a binary, as well as an imagined suppressive force that she seeks to expose. The real question is whether this ontological logic was *forceful* as such in the first place. None of the Abrahamic traditions 'succeed' at monotheism, Schneider claims (Schneider 2008, 204). Given her absolutist and 'totalitarian' understanding of monotheism, however, it is not quite convincing that these traditions tried to achieve monotheism in her sense. At points when she is trying to illustrate the alternative to the logic of the One, she refers to figures of thought that are internal to the traditions she claims are dominated by this logic. For example, she claims that multiplicity 'is what happens when something is more than the sum of its parts but also, by virtue of its necessary

---

[28] Schneider relies on Gilles Deleuze's philosophy at a number of points in the book, especially when explicating her ontological position. See Schneider (2008, 128).

participation as a part of other somethings, is not itself therefore completely whole' (Schneider 2008, 143). Yet, it seems that such a figure cannot be said to explode or break open an iron cage of received wisdom as much as it exemplifies an aporia that many of the philosophical and religious traditions on trial in her book have continued to ponder.[29]

Schneider's approach beckons further troubles. First, by reducing monotheism to the ideological expression of the logic of the One, she disregards wideranging tendencies to multiplicity in monotheistic traditions as either not multiple enough or as deviations from monotheism. On a purely logical level, this suggests, as with Assmann, that her definition is neither sufficiently precise nor relevant enough.

Second, Schneider claims that forces of oppression, such as racism, nationalism, ethnocentrism, and so forth, intertwine, which would seem to necessitate a more encompassing theory of our current difficulties. I nonetheless submit that framing the problem as the logic of the One may erase the particularity of oppression as much as it sheds light on it (Schneider 2008, 3). Insofar as dynamics of oppression intersect and intertwine, we surely need to approach oppression as a highly complex phenomenon. However, the identification of monotheism with empire, monarchy, totalitarianism, racism, and so on, makes a real critique of oppression almost impossible from this vantage point. Every instance of unity is potentially a product of the logic of the One, and so potentially totalitarian or imperialist. Her genealogy conjures deep pathos since the logic of the One is infinite and the victims of monotheism everywhere. Inversely, every 'posture' or 'gesture' of multiplicity can be viewed as potentially liberatory. Thus, it is precisely because Schneider inscribes monotheism in a highly abstract meta-theory of violence that she is unable to explain the particularities of monotheistic violence.

Third, I have argued that a modern European concern with the exclusion of religion as a source of violence and political unrest frames the discourse on monotheism. I believe Schneider perpetuates some of these themes, and her explanation of the causes of monotheism follows quite traditional lines. In the wake of 9/11, Schneider's book exemplifies a broader tendency to search for the religious causes of violence. Hans G. Kippenberg writes that the attack on the World Trade Center was 'perceived in the light of a liberal political discourse that was marked by the memory of the violence in Europe after the Reformation' (Kippenberg 2020, 21). By repeating such oppositions, she perpetuates the Enlightenment contention that religious beliefs underwritten by fear are the primary driver of violence. Reminiscent of Hume, she claims

---

[29] See, for example, Booth (1983).

that oneness is 'rooted in a psychology of scarcity' (Schneider 2008, 136). Monotheism is a reaction to insecurity, a shortcut to a stable world for subjects threatened merely linked with deeply problematic regimes of power; it is reductive to the logic of those regimes. Monotheism is not 'extricable from monarchical and supremacist entailments' on the individual or collective level. Christian monotheism is 'an empty concept in itself, apart from these entailments' (Schneider 2008, 26).

Despite these criticisms, I appreciate Schneider's focus on the incarnation as a locus for thinking about the politics of monotheism. She helpfully turns central Christian beliefs about revelation into an opportunity for thinking both about the limits of human conceptual and practical mastery. Put in different terms, precisely that place where God seems, for the Enlightenment critique of religion, to be reduced to a mere 'fact' of history, and thus where the One God seems to be definitively represented unequivocally, Schneider seeks to unsettle the determinations of thought. Schneider addresses a dangerous tendency in Christian monotheism to turn Christ into the source of an authority that rules over, yet also divides, the world. In representing Christ, who represents God, Christians may come to represent themselves as carriers of a communal power whose very operation is to include those who fit and excise those who do not. This is, of course, a genuine danger for Christian political theology. That is why Schneider would instead think of the incarnation as an iconoclastic occurrence. There is no 'correct' identification of God, only the monotheistic tendency to search for one – which is, itself, the clearest form of idolatry. In denying the representability of Jesus' body, Schneider absolutises the prohibition against images to such an extent that almost *any* representation of God amounts to idolatry. Effectively, then, idolatry is all around. Still, the Mosaic distinction, the division between 'us' and 'them' that both Assmann and Schneider find so problematic, is rendered inoperative by her theology of multiplicity. The theology of multiplicity implies that 'our' God cannot be selected or circumscribed so as to reject the gods of others.

Nevertheless, monotheism does not seem to be quite the universal danger that Schneider makes it out to me. In short, she reads more into monotheism than is warranted, as I have suggested. It seems that instead of dealing with the particularity of the divine is represented and what its political effects may be, she condemns without warrant – for how could such a condemnation be warranted? – all representation as such. By pitting the incarnation against the logic of the One, she effaces a fruitful resource for reflecting on the relationship between idolatry and representation in the Christian tradition.

Schneider thus leaves no room for the notion that the incarnation is a form of representation or, to return to the Pauline phrase – that the Son is the image of the invisible God. Without this notion, however, it is hard to make sense of the Christian belief in Jesus Christ. This particular body – the body of Jesus – was always already interpreted, represented, and exchanged in the many narratives, liturgies, practices, traditions, and stories that inscribed this body into memory – that made it, in other words, accessible to us (Ward 2005, 29–59). These narratives of the particular body have been perpetuated by the very same churches that have believed in the doctrine of the incarnation. Theologically speaking, as I have noted, Christians have believed that the Church is tasked with this work of representation by being incorporated into – and thus extending – Christ's body.

Throughout history, people have naturally proposed a wide range of interpretations of what it actually means to give witness to Jesus Christ, and thus to represent the One True God. Assmann claims that the coming of the Messiah is thought to 'revoke' the distinction between Jew and Gentile, so as to universalise the Mosaic distinction (Assmann 2005, 155; 2010, 17). With this, however, comes the possibility of saying (in contrast with what he believes was the practice of Israel) that any single person *ought* to be on God's side but has somehow chosen not to and so stand in opposition to God's truth.

In his book *Monotheism, Intolerance, and the Path to Pluralistic Politics,* Christopher A. Haw observes that Assmann is surprisingly vague about what the truth of monotheism, Christianity or otherwise, consists of (Haw 2021, 189). Haw calls for caution at this point, for the range of interpretations of the faith in Jesus Christ and their political effects are both varied and not seldom worrisome. Haw notes that a common way to understand this faith, in line with much historical Christianity from Constantine onwards, is to present Christ as the ultimate monarch, who, through an 'ultimate sacrifice', founds a new Kingdom that supersedes yet also fulfils 'archaic religio-polities' (Haw 2021, 193). Traditional Christian political theology is, in other words, a form of tribalism that considers itself universal. The problem with this theology, Haw believes, is that the benevolent and radically peaceful aspects of Jesus' message are inevitably displaced to private morality, while the exigencies of power relativise that message in the political sphere.

Haw notes that the other alternative that has existed throughout history is a radically non-institutional theology, where the truth of Christ is a truth not of this world – a radically inclusive vision that nonetheless sheds particularities and identities (Haw 2021, 192). This is Christian monotheism transformed into a universalist ethic of inclusion, confessing no position and thus no enemies. The first case is domineering and imperialist; the second is professedly inclusivist but hides its particularistic intolerance. In each case, Christians have proposed a particular sociopolitical identity that, wittingly or unwittingly, masks the violence needed to achieve its coherence.

Haw employs René Girard's theories of mimetic desire and the human propensity to select scapegoats to end society's vicious circle of violence. According to Girard, human identity arises through a logic of desire that is inherently *mimetic*: humans choose their goals, and thus their identities, not because they naturally want them, but because they see other people wanting them. As a result, desire, and therefore identity, is entangled in a logic of inescapable competition and, ultimately, violence. The way that human societies have dealt with the cycles of violence that thus ensues is to select a scapegoat on which the ultimate blame is shifted. For both Haw and Girard, violence is inherently ambivalent: while it is destructive, violence is also used as a form of containment against further violence (Haw 2021, 129).

For Haw, following Girard, Jesus Christ's uniqueness consists in being the divine sacrificial victim who reveals and subverts the scapegoating mechanism.[30] To give witness to the crucifixion of God is to recognise that we are all responsible for victim-making, that we are the perpetrators who would have killed God (Haw 2021, 240). The first truth of Jesus Christ, then, is a truth about us, that we are the ones who constantly need to define ourselves in opposition to and put the blame on the other. By revealing this, however, Christ turns the Mosaic distinction on its head, Haw notes. The 'other' of the Christian identity is not the heathen, it is not those who refuse to worship 'our God' – it is instead Christ as a victim of our violence. Christ unmasks the violence of our mimetic desire. Thus, Golgatha, the cross, 'is Sinai's interpretive key' (Haw 2021, 242). The Mosaic distinction is revealed as the product of our own hatred. If this is true, the faith in Jesus Christ helps us see that politics is 'sacred', not in a positive way, but as marked by the ambiguity of all sacrifice. This ambiguity characterises all societies insofar as they, without exception, presuppose a founding murder.

May we hope, however, for a truth beyond violence-containment, or is the faith in Jesus Christ but a confirmation our violence, of the all-pervasive nature of the Mosaic distinction? The ultimate truth of Jesus Christ, Haw claims following Girard, is in some sense silent. There is, in other words, no privileged access to the absolute, no position from which the 'right' ordering of life can be gleaned and put into effect. Instead, God's truth is the truth of the victims, the voice of those who are always being effaced (Haw 2021, 241–42). Consequently, idolatry is no longer defined as images of false gods but the violent tendency of all of us to hate the God of love. Inversely, true representation is only possible as a kind of anti-representation, namely as the 'destroyed image of God, Christ crucified' (Haw 2021, 242). It follows, then, that the Church, which is tasked with representing

---

[30] Girard developed these theories throughout his works, but a key work is Girard, Oughourlian, and Lefort (2016).

this crucified God, can only exist as a subject by giving up its right to exist in a privileged position, subsisting only as the founding victim, the 'non-instantiable pressure of critique against every earthly city' (Haw 2021, 249).

I believe there is much to admire about Haw's Girardian reading of how Jesus Christ transforms the Mosaic distinction and enables a wholly different kind of monotheism. He rightly points out that Christian monotheism need not entail 'believing or pretending "as if" there is a big One God (and that we are, of course, on "his side")' (Haw 2021, 250). For the gravity entailed by God's judgement is not, contrary to Assmann's Mosaic distinction, that 'we' stand on the side of truth and others on the side of untruth. As Herbert McCabe once wrote, we 'do *not* have "God on our side", and this is not because God is neutral but because we are compromised' (McCabe 2005, 79). This is not to say that believers have not, at innumerable times, claimed to be standing on the right side of God's judgement, but only to say that the Christian traditions (not wholly unlike other monotheistic traditions) are full of symbols, narratives, and discourses that challenge any such claim. Haw, therefore, rightly shows how the belief in the incarnation of God in Christ can contribute to the questioning of Christian supremacy.

Another way of saying this – and I am not directly building on Haw here – is that Christian faith puts pressure on any representation of the divine, including those it recognises as 'its own'. This 'apophatic' impulse in Christian practice and reflection is not merely a gesture to the limits of representation – even if it is that, too. It is not simply to do with the limits of our concepts, as if God is an object 'out there' that we do not have access to. Speech about the divine is speech in response to a divine activity that initially determines the subject and its context; it is a limit of language and expression that follows just as much from immersion as distance (Williams 2023). Thus, Ruggieri claims, commenting on idolatry in Christian monotheism', that the 'central problem of discourse on God is not that of making God known, but of purifying ourselves so that we can stand in his presence. This presence of God can be grasped only through a process of transcending, of *ekstasis*, with regard to all conceptual habits' (Ruggieri 1985, 21). This is why Karen Kilby is critical of Social Trinitarianism, which seeks to say that a particular understanding of the Trinity may inspire a certain kind of politics. If we turn a certain representation of God into a conceptual model of religious truth to be imitated, we treat religious truth as primarily something that is being performed by the subject – as if human thoughts may perfectly 'grasp' the divine – as if God can be 'a kind of intellectual object over which I dispose' (Kilby 2020, 53). The implication of this approach is that living in truth is to live in a dominant relationship with the world and the other, that knowledge is ultimately a form of power, a way of making the other disposable.

Jan Assmann's claim that monotheism creates a distinction between true and false worship that, translated into political life, turns into a distinction between friend and enemy is only possible if 'God' as such can be unequivocally determined. Yet, speaking truthfully about God is not necessarily about picking the right 'regulative concept' as much as it is speaking of a reality in which we are already involved and that questions our own desire for mastery and independence (Bauerschmidt 2011). The Jewish theologian Franz Rosenzweig argued, against the modern identification of idolatry with transcendental illusion, that the first commandment (or, second, as in the Talmud) does not reject images as such, but only *graven* images (Batnitzky 2000, 23–25). In other words, the source of idolatry is the very human act of *fixing* images, making permanent and universally validated representations of God that 'work' at any time and place. The problem with idolatry is, in other words, to think of the representation of the divine as a predictable operation, something that either 'works' or does not work, and thus as something I can master if only I perform the operations correctly. Rosenzweig thought that the problem with such images is that they deny God's freedom to be represented yet also to escape representation. Assmann rightly sees that monotheistic notions of God stress his unique character, yet he does not sufficiently acknowledge that, for many Christians and people of other monotheistic faiths, this character challenges their self-sufficiency in knowing that they are on the 'right' side. Haw's discussion of Christian monotheism admirably stresses this very point.

However, I believe that both Schneider and Haw stray too far into portraying any form of representation of Jesus Christ as a form of idolatry. While Haw believes that the Mosaic distinction between true and false worship is necessary, its role is to remind us of our own tendency to destroy others in the name of 'our' true God. Like Schneider, Haw seeks to counter the hegemonic claim of a monotheism that undergirds a unity of power, one that is inevitably set against antagonistic others. However, his Girardian reading of Christology (as well as his use of Chantal Mouffe) entails that the Mosaic distinction, the antagonism between 'us' and 'them' is a constitutive feature of political experience. The violence of politics is, in a sense, necessary for our understanding of Christian monotheism because Jesus' role is precisely to reveal the logic of violence in political life – and in ourselves. For that reason, the Church does not transcend antagonism to occupy a universal and peaceable space. It can only exist as a force that questions particular identities that portray themselves as universal while effacing their own violence.

I fully agree that Christianity can only carry any hope of being peaceable if it questions its own idea of itself as a universal peaceable 'space', as if it has transcended political antagonism and violence. Furthermore, there is no denying the innumerable institutionalised and politicised modes of defending the Church throughout history. Haw is right to look to the manifold practices in the Christian tradition that question its tendency to 'defend' its message or institutionalised way of life. At the same time, such self-critical strands of Christian monotheism have been linked with an effort to represent Jesus Christ in a faithful manner – that is, by faithfully living 'in' the Body of Christ. To represent Christ for the Church is to be a witness of a community of unrestricted solidarity. This community has no need of a distinction because it has no self-interest to defend. To live in such a state of perfect solidarity is, of course, impossible – which is precisely why it sits uneasily with earthly rule.

For Christians, being incorporated in the Body of Christ has meant partaking in a community that seeks to represent – make present – Jesus Christ, the image of the invisible God. This kind of representation, furthermore, is material, social, and political on various levels. It institutes a whole range of relations among peoples that are very real and that, therefore, are always caught up in the webs of negotiation, hostility, and domination that always attend social life. Ever since St Paul said that there were neither Jew nor Gentile (Gal 3:28), Christians have thought of their way of life as something that transcends other identities and communities. This is the very reason why, politically speaking, Christianity introduced the distinction between *temporal* and *spiritual* powers. As with Schneider, it has led critics of representation, Giorgio Agamben being another example, to believe that Christianity may a subversive or indifferent relationship to every identity (Agamben 2005). However, it seems that Christianity traditionally has spoken of the Christian life as something at least partly legible in terms of human subjectivity, desire, and goal-making. The Christian life is an attempt to represent both the human and the divine in a particular way.

Christian representation is essentially communal; it would not make sense without at least some legitimate collective practices that seek to represent God in particular ways. However, precisely because theological representations are subject to God's judgement, the community and its individuals often fail in their representation. Indeed, the repertoire of early Christian encounters with the divine is full of failed encounters or representations – Peter's denial of Christ, the wanderers at Emmaus, Saul's persecution of Christ, and Augustine's befuddled search for a God that was always there. Indeed, such stories have so shaped the Christian language of representation that, in the words of Williams, the apophatic negation of Christian god-talk is not to do with 'a set of fixed general principles but the articulating of particular histories of encounter, response and verbal/conceptual frustration' (Williams 2023, 5).

The very possibility of failure, however, assumes that there are some human practices that may be said to be faithful to God on at least some level. My objection to Haw is that the Girardian understanding of violence equates the political with violence-containment and ultimately can only find a tangential relationship between faith and political life in this sense. Haw stresses that the Gospel is both 'dialectical' and 'analogical', for it is not to do with a Kingdom of another world but reveals itself in the victim of *this* world. However, it nonetheless leaves an impression of this world as primarily constituted by violence. By contrast, Haw claims, Christ, the wholly different king, 'speaks a language the political cannot speak; for it speaks through its being expelled by the political' (Haw 2021, 214). Both Schneider's ontology and Girard's theory of mimetic desire, on which Haw builds, portray identity – and the processes by which we represent the identities of ourselves, of the other, and of the divine – as constituted by violence. Thus, according to John Milbank, Girard risks 'lodging sin gnostically in our finitude' (Milbank 1995, 42). In fact, where Assmann ultimately hopes to separate 'religion' as a peaceful force against the violence of politics, Girard unites politics and the sacred in a sacrificial logic that can only be indirectly questioned by the victim of its violence.

I do not wish to deny the violence in politics but to challenge the assumption that the divine can only wreak havoc when somehow imitated in political life. It should be said, however, that Haw does not believe that Jesus is a wholly non-political figure. Jesus' silence in face of Pilates is a 'silent-judgement from the position of the judged', and so directly bears on the political: 'This "king" speaks a language the political cannot speak; for it speaks through its being expelled by the political. Instead of rendering a new judgment, Christ's judgment unsettles all judgment' (Haw 2021, 214). Thus, Jesus' monotheism does not mean 'some depoliticizes transcending of the violence of the political' (Haw 2021, 215).

So, more than Schneider, Haw recognises the necessity of concrete Christian practice and witness: 'So long as we live in a world of hubris and victimization, we cannot abrogate the representation of solid images of land, victims, and collective identification' (Haw 2021, 233). Christian practice is, therefore, political. Thus, he notes, for example, how Martin Luther King Jr. sought to provoke a sociopolitical crisis through his practice of non-violence (Haw 2021, 242). For Haw, King's non-violent politics illustrates of how Christian witness can be politically subversive.

While I do not disagree with that claim, I think his reference to King highlights where I disagree. Haw quotes King defending his movement's potential for causing conflict by saying that 'We merely bring to the surfaces the hidden tension that is already alive'. My worry about this claim, at least as an expression of a more general theological position, is that the only possible political 'gesture' grounded in Jesus Christ is that of siding with the victim who *reveals* the violence of political representation. In other words, the only legitimate form of religious representation is the one that exposes the brokenness of all revelation.

Thus, contrary to both Schneider and Haw, I resist the claim that faith can only be redeemed as a challenge to representation as such – be it political or religious. The problem, I believe, is a deep-seated instinct, inherited from the Enlightenment discourse of religion and politics – that there must be some *general explanation* (ontological or epistemological) of religious violence that would allow us to efface the violence of religious representation. This instinct, I suggest, is turned into a theology whereby Jesus Christ is only imaginable as a destroyer of all images, or, as for Haw, as an image of the 'destroyed image of God'.

I believe that the 'silence' of Jesus Christ that Schneider rightly highlighted is not the body's general resistance against any and all forms of representation. It is, instead, the resistance against a particular kind of authority, against the implicit and explicit violence in this political life at this point in time. It is not that speaking up would, as such, be a kind of compromise of the body's silent multiplicity; it is rather that speaking up to justify oneself in the face of this concrete example of authoritarian political rule would jeopardise the attempt to represent another kind of authority not dependent on the need to demarcate one's own territory. I cannot, of course, establish the validity of my interpretation here, but only put it forward as quite a common position that Schneider excludes on ontological grounds. This alternative is simply that Jesus' life can be interpreted as a protest and rejection of the violence in political and religious representations, without it being an absolute rejection of politics and representation.

The Church's existence in this world is inescapably political: it seeks to represent the divine in the world, it represents the world to itself, and it represents the world to God. For that very reason, it is fully enmeshed in human negotiation, conflict, and self-defence. Yet, I am simply highlighting that its tradition harbours a logic of representation that also pushes against the sense that the God it seeks to represent is 'owned' by the Church, that it stands on the right side of God's judgement, or that it inhabits a protected and peaceful 'space' in the world.

To sum up, what I am arguing is that in recent significant discussions of Christian monotheism, there lingers an attempt to seek a general explanation and resolution to the Christian politics of monotheism and that this explanation is centred around the logic of representation as bound to the Christian faith in Jesus Christ. These discussions do, in themselves, point to the fact that there are decisive resources in the Christian tradition for challenging an antagonistic understanding of faith. However, contrary to the thinkers discussed here, I have sought to press the point that there is no *general* way of escaping the violence of representation – for there is no *general* violence of representation;

no *general* violence of the rejection of idolatry. There is no necessary, but plenty of actual cases of violence in identifying of true ways of living in God's truth. Put in different terms, the Enlightenment inheritance in contemporary critiques of monotheism tends to lead to a worry that there is something inherently or potentially violent about representing the divine in the world – that it is, as such, a dangerous act.

My point is that it is not at all clear that it is the general act of representation as such that is the problem. This is not a very original point, and it would not be necessary to make, were it not that contemporary debates of the politics of monotheism tend to reiterate conceptual frameworks from the Enlightenment that do not fit with how theological language is understood in major monotheistic traditions. Thus, as I will expand in the final section, these reflections do not seek to 'excuse' monotheism from the violence committed in the name of the One God. If anything, they challenge Christians and others who confess the One God to owning up to the often-troubling politics of monotheism.

7 The Politics of Monotheism

The critiques of the politics of monotheism I have considered in this Element all echo concrete political experiences: the term 'monotheism' itself arose and played an equivocal role in an early modern Europe fractured and distressed by the political and religious wars after the Reformation; Peterson and Moltmann saw the long legacy of monotheism in the totalitarian regimes of the twentieth century. For them, monotheism legitimated and encouraged consolidation of power in a single ruler. Schneider and Assmann both wrote about monotheism in a globalised world haunted by theses about clashes of civilisation. They wrote works that attend the post-9/11 world and sought solidarity and community beyond the representations of bounded national communities or groups. Where Assmann used concepts inherited from the Enlightenment to challenge claims of absolute truth, Schneider employed recent continental philosophy to critique the logic of the One. All of these thinkers, however, shared the idea that monotheism is somehow to blame for a particular kind of violence, unjustified political rule, or for instigating political antagonisms. Their worries echo Jean-Luc Nancy's worry that an ambivalent relationship with absolute truth haunts contemporary political life.

The political experiences of these thinkers marked their theological critiques of monotheism. Peterson and Moltmann were concerned that the unity of God could be seen to be repeated by the one Emperor. For Peterson, any such analogy between divine and earthly rulership was problematic, while for Moltmann, there remained a possibility for analogy, although quite a different one. However, we saw that these discussions about the Trinity and monotheism were tied up with the doctrine of the incarnation because the incarnation opens the path to a divine sanction of certain representations of God and thus to legitimating certain political regimes as expressions or imitations of the divine. As we moved to Schneider's critique of monotheism, we saw that her critique goes further in postulating monotheism as a theological expression of an all-pervasive logic, a doggedly persistent fall into a reduction of multiplicity into oneness. Her solution is unorthodox, even as it centres on the key Christian doctrine of the incarnation.

What I have argued in the Element is that the notion of monotheism is part of a modern discourse of religion that seeks to identify the religious origins of violence and political conflict. Despite their difference, Assmann, Peterson, Moltmann, and Schneider share the conviction that monotheism is politically worrisome at best. I have sought to show that such a strategy involves constructing an abstraction that does not really conform to the great monotheistic traditions. Furthermore, I have suggested that the confession to the absolute truth cannot be understood without reflecting on the prohibition against images. In other words, the relationship between God and creation and its implied consequence for theological knowledge is essential to understanding the nature of idolatry.

Contrary to the hopes grounded in the Enlightenment fear of religious violence, I believe there is no way, based on formal considerations alone, to guarantee that the politics of monotheism may be either beneficial or harmful. From a Christian theological perspective, this is because the relationship between God and creation can only be represented through a material reflection on the incarnation. In other words, the Christian confession to the absolute truth is inextricable from an interpretation of the concrete human-divine activities narrated, represented, and refined in the Christian traditions of reflection on the life of Jesus Christ. From the point of view of Christian theology, only through these reflections can one get a sense of what it would mean to truly 'represent', and thus confess, the one true God – as well as what it would mean *not* to represent God. It is through this reflection and practice of representation that one may gain a sense of the monotheistic politics of Christianity.

However, such a position underscores the severe *risk* that attains to Christian reflection and practice. The abstract claim that there is only One True God is neither inherently benign nor bad. It is, however, a central part of Christianity, and it is deeply entangled with the political cultures influenced by Christianity as well as other traditions. And yet, the political cultures growing out of the early modern European religious and political experience have a deeply ambivalent attitude towards monotheism. This history has contributed to the conviction that political life must be shielded from religious dogmatism or 'positivity', lest violence break out. Religion is seen as making political life antagonistic and irreconcilable, undermining the 'translation' of viewpoints and civilised discussions about truth or values.

Part of this inheritance from the Enlightenment is the worry about any complicity with religious sources of violence. The eagerness among secular and Christian thinkers to expose monotheism as a culprit indicates that we have yet to overcome the tensions of religion and politics, or transcendence and immanence, which is part of a religio-political history formed by the great monotheistic traditions. These tensions, which were so deeply felt in the long wake of the Reformation, have led many thinkers to search for a theory of violence that might help us exclude it from political life. However, this can only be done by abstracting 'violence' from what Gillian Rose calls 'the broken middle' – the aporetic and difficult situation of human life caught between transcendence and immanence, or domination and freedom (Rose 1992, xii).

Such attempts amount to futile attempts to make representation 'safe', to delimit the space of possible truth claims. In this way, the rejection of monotheism betrays the ambivalence of authority in modern political life. Out of this modern ambivalence comes the inverse kind of discourse, which is the legacy of the rejection of idolatry in modern European thought. As we have seen, after the Enlightenment, some thinkers thought that a kind of 'pure monotheism' – untied from the positivity of revelation and dogma – was necessary for both moral and political life. As this idea was translated into epistemological terms after Kant, 'monotheism' could be understood as a figure for the limits of knowledge, yet also play an ethical role. Idolatry, in this context, is defined in epistemological and ideological terms.

In modern philosophy, then, *critique* is the legacy of the first commandment. The neo-Kantian philosopher Hermann Cohen (1842–1918) claimed that the prohibition against images was Judaism's chief philosophical contribution. This rejection of idolatry has persisted in modern European thought, from Heidegger's destruction of metaphysics to Jürgen Habermas' communicative reason, Giorgio Agamben's critique of sovereign power, or the radical democrats' insistence that the sovereign centre of politics is 'empty' (Agamben 1998; Laclau and Mouffe 2001; Lefort 2006; Habermas 2019).

My argument in this Element has been that we need to think of the politics of monotheism not only as a distinction between absolute truth and false truth, but as also as consisting of a wide variety of ways in which that truth is represented. To that extent, the modern transposition of iconoclasm to critique is essential, since it concerns precisely the question of representation. However, the issue with post-Kantian critique is that, as Rose argues, by refusing to 'think the absolute' – that is, by interpreting the commandment as a refusal of all images, a new series of dichotomies arise (Rose 2009). A purely apophatic monotheism would seem to lead to a critical approach to all political projects – for none can be said to 'represent' the divine. Yet, the outcome of that approach would be that monotheism's only contribution to politics is to efface any implicit theology, thus contributing to the notion that politics is primarily the field of violence.

If one follows this line of critique, the imagined positive alternative can only reappear as a post-representational ethics, as an intimation of the good without authority or representation. Thus, as a Jewish philosopher, Rose also criticised modern and postmodern Jewish philosophy – as with Walter Benjamin or Emmanuel Levinas – for turning Judaism into a pure ethic, just as she criticised Christian thinkers for turning to a wordless gospel of love (Rose 1996, 85; 1992). I believe similar criticisms could also be made of Schneider's and Haw's theological proposals.

For such reasons, I am sceptical towards attempts to rule out all representations of the One God or to translate the legacy of monotheism into the rejection of representation as such. While the modern epistemological transformation of the first commandment presents a *univocal* means of identifying idolatry (because *any* attempt to represent the absolute is idolatrous), I believe, drawing on resources of Christian traditions, that the processes of identifying and rejecting idolatry are both more uncertain and more concrete than that. A Christian approach to idolatry has to do with certain practices of identification, affirmation, and disavowals that cannot be made according to formalised rules but rather demand the plotted narratives from which the Christian confession to truth arises.

What, then, should we say about the politics of monotheism? If we approach the politics of monotheism on an empirical level, as part of a sociological study, or as part of a comparative study of religion, I remain decidedly agnostic (yet open) about the results: what monotheism is or entails, depends so much on context, that it is impossible to make a universal judgement from a putatively 'objective' position.[31] Thus, I am tentatively sceptical that there is a single 'politics of monotheism' that might be analysed and identified across time and space. This is not to reject the term monotheism as a descriptive term but only to say that it does not hold much explanatory power on its own.

There is no need to let monotheism off the hook. Monotheism might very well contribute to violence or legitimate dangerous political ideologies. Expressions of faith are always part of negotiations of human life that may become dangerous and are often implicated in witting and unwitting violence. Yet, I do not believe it is possible to abstract monotheism as a univocal

---

[31] See one such attempt in Stark (2003).

distinction, belief, or logic from the great monotheistic traditions from which we can deduce probable political consequences.

It follows from what I have said that any discussion of the politics of monotheism must remain concrete. For followers of monotheistic traditions, and as in my case, for those who identify with Christian traditions, I believe one ought to recognise how, in very concrete terms, one's confession to the One True God has functioned in history, for both good and bad. To recognise this is to acknowledge one's implication in the violence, and in this case, the violence of absolute truth. Acknowledging one's implication in violence is not to value nor reject the possibility of change but to admit that there is no way of imagining a peaceable life – with other human beings, nature, or God – without a real risk for instigating new violence.

I believe we need to take responsibility for the violence of our traditions but also discover – theological and otherwise – the resources for other ways of acting socially and politically. In a common turn of phrase, Giuseppe Ruggieri has claimed that 'it is not monotheism as such, but a particular *use* of it that makes it a function of a view of society in which order and the common good are assured by a sovereign will' (Ruggieri 1985, 21). I follow Ruggieri, with the exception that I do not believe such a claim turns monotheism into an inherently good thing – precisely because I am, on theological grounds, suspicious of proclaiming *any* representations of God innocent as such.

Nonetheless, in owning up to history's misuse of monotheism, one might also begin to search for better uses. Some may think such a reparative approach tiresome or hypocritical – for how long can theologians continue to reinterpret past doctrine and claim that it means something other than what it meant? As I have argued, one should certainly not deny the violent potential in monotheism – and yet, the particularity of violence can also be effaced by an abstract concept of monotheism. Furthermore, to reinterpret monotheistic traditions and speak of a more 'authentic' monotheism is necessary precisely because it is an act of taking responsibility. In trying to discover a more authentic monotheism, one is also able to take responsibility for 'false' monotheisms. Implicating oneself in a tradition must always involve sharing the burdens and responsibilities produced by its failures.

Thus, I submit we must search for the politics of monotheism 'from within', just as all politics and all theology must be sought within. Comparative research into the ideas and practices of monotheistic traditions is very valuable, but they must not halt the process of negotiation, critique, and self-critique that various monotheistic traditions harbour. Identifying and excluding sources of violence is certainly part of that process, but it is far from everything. From a Christian perspective, I believe one must conclude that truth cannot be effaced completely from politics, even if one must limit the scope of the politics of truth. Christian traditions of political life extend and transform the critique of political idolatry in their own fashion. Through their faith in Jesus Christ, they hallow time and matter as sacred, all the while emphasising that temporal political life cannot be fully disclosive of the truth. Part of what a Church does, for Christians, is, in and through Jesus Christ, to represent sacred time so that what is gained and lost – of truth, resource, and life – in ordinary time is both relativised, transformed, and directed towards the future of all things. There is a politics of truth in the Christian tradition, and it resonates with other monotheisms in relating truth to political life.

Was Jean-Luc Nancy right, then, that Western societies struggle with their relationship to the truth? Yes, and I have sought to show why the large monotheistic traditions play an indispensable role in the story about that relationship. I do not, however, believe that we can think of monotheism as such as really the problem or the solution to our struggles. Instead, we must own up to the responsibility and risk of representing truth in political life, whether we are people of faith or not. The story of Jesus may tell us what may be at stake when we do so.

References

Agamben, Giorgio. 1998. *Homo Sacer: Sovereign Power and Bare Life.* Translated by Daniel Heller-Roazen. Meridian. Stanford, CA: Stanford University Press.

2005. *The Time That Remains: A Commentary on the Letter to the Romans.* Translated by Patricia Dailey. Stanford, CA: Stanford University Press.

Asad, Talal. 1999. 'Religion, Nation-State, Secularism'. In *Nation and Religion: Perspectives on Europe and Asia,* edited by Peter van der Veer and Hartmut Lehmann, 178–96. Princeton: Princeton University Press.

2003. *Formations of the Secular: Christianity, Islam, Modernity.* Stanford: Stanford University Press.

Assmann, Jan. 1997. *Moses the Egyptian: The Memory of Egypt in Western Monotheism.* Cambridge, MA: Harvard University Press.

1998. *Moses der Ägypter: Entzifferung einer Gedächtnisspur.* München: C. Hanser.

2000. *Herrschaft und Heil: politische Theologie in Altägypten, Israel und Europa.* München: C. Hanser.

2003. *Die mosaische Unterscheidung, oder, Der Preis des Monotheismus.* München: Carl Hanser.

2005. 'Monotheism and Its Political Consequences'. In *Religion and Politics,* edited by Daniel Šuber and Bernhard Giesen, 3:141–59. London: Brill. https://doi.org/10.11588/propylaeumdok.00003424.

2008. *Of God and Gods: Egypt, Israel, and the Rise of Monotheism.* Madison, WI: University of Wisconsin Press.

2010. *The Price of Monotheism.* Stanford: Stanford University Press.

2014. *Religio Duplex: How the Enlightenment Reinvented Egyptian Religion.* Translated by Robert Savage. Cambridge: Polity Press.

2016. *From Akhenaten to Moses: Ancient Egypt and Religious Change.* Cairo: The American University in Cairo Press.

Bakunin, Michael. 1970. *God and the State.* New York: Dover.

Balagangadhara, S. N. 1994. *The Heathen in His Blindness: Asia, the West and the Dynamic of Religion.* Leiden: Brill.

Ballentine, Debra Scoggins. 2022. '"Monotheism" and the Hebrew Bible'. *Religion Compass* 16 (1). https://doi.org/10.1111/rec3.12425.

Batnitzky, Leora. 2000. *Idolatry and Representation: The Philosophy of Franz Rosenzweig Reconsidered.* Princeton: Princeton University Press.

Bauckham, Richard. 1981. 'The Worship of Jesus in Apocalyptic Christianity'. *New Testament Studies* 27 (3): 322–41. https://doi.org/10.1017/S00286885 00006718.

Bauerschmidt, Frederick Christian. 2011. 'The Trinity and Politics'. In *The Oxford Handbook of the Trinity*, edited by Gilles Emery and Matthew Levering, 531–44. Oxford: Oxford University Press.

Benedikter, Roland. 2023. 'The Role of Religion in Russia's Ukraine War. Part 2: Developments and Perspectives'. *Zeitschrift Für Außen- Und Sicherheitspolitik* 16 (2): 173–98. https://doi.org/10.1007/s12399-023-00947-7.

Benson, Bruce Ellis. 2002. *Graven Ideologies: Nietzsche, Derrida & Marion on Modern Idolatry*. Downers Grove, IL: InterVarsity Press.

Bergem, Ragnar M. 2017. 'On the Persistence of the Genealogical in Contemporary Theology'. *Modern Theology* 33 (3): 434–52.

——— 2019. *Politisk teologi*. Oslo: Dreyers forlag.

——— 2023. 'The Spirit of Modernity and Its Fate'. *Modern Theology* 39: 640–65, February. https://doi.org/10.1111/moth.12850.

Berman, Harold Joseph. 2003. *Law and Revolution, II: The Impact of the Protestant Reformations on the Western Legal Tradition*. Cambridge, MA: The Belknap press of Harvard university press.

Besançon, Alain. 2000. *The Forbidden Image: An Intellectual History of Iconoclasm*. Chicago: University of Chicago Press.

Boff, Leonardo. 1988. *Trinity and Society*. Maryknoll, NY: Orbis Books.

——— 2000. *Holy Trinity, Perfect Community*. Maryknoll, NY: Orbis Books.

Bolingbroke, Henry St. John Lord Viscount. 1756. *The Works of the Late Right Honourable Henry St. John, Lord Viscount Bolingbroke*. Vol. 2. London.

Booth, Edward. 1983. *Aristotelian Aporetic Ontology in Islamic and Christian Thinkers*. Cambridge: Cambridge University Press.

Brito Vieira, Mónica, and David Runciman. 2008. *Representation*. Cambridge: Polity.

Broughton, Thomas. 1732. *Christianity Distinct from the Religion of Nature*. London: Weaver Bickerton.

Buckley, Michael J. 1990. *At the Origins of Modern Atheism*. New Haven, CT: Yale University Press.

Bunzel, Cole. 2015. 'From Paper State to Caliphate: The Ideology of the Islamic State'. The Brookings Project on U.S. Relations with the Islamic World.

Byrne, Peter. 2015. *Natural Religion and the Nature of Religion: The Legacy of Deism*. London: Routledge.

Cavanaugh, William T. 2004. 'Killing for the Telephone Company: Why the Nation-State Is Not the Keeper of the Common Good'. *Modern Theology* 20 (2): 243–74. https://doi.org/10.1111/j.1468-0025.2004.00252.x.

——— 2009. *The Myth of Religious Violence: Secular Ideology and the Roots of Modern Conflict*. Oxford: Oxford University Press.

Coakley, Sarah. 2021. 'Beyond Understanding'. *Political Theology* 22 (5): 398–406. https://doi.org/10.1080/1462317X.2021.1955575.

Colpe, Carsten. 2007. 'Monotheismus'. In *Fragen Nach Dem Einen Gott: Die Monotheismusdebatte Im Kontext*, edited by Gesine Palmer, 23–27. Tübingen: Mohr Siebeck.

Connolly, William E. 1999. *Why I Am Not a Secularist*. Minneapolis, MN: University of Minnesota Press.

Corneri, Davidis Gregorii. 1642. *Vita D. N. Jesu Christi Divino-Humana; Eiusq. Virgineae Matris Mariae*. Vienna: Gregorii Gelbhaar.

Demacopoulos, George E. 2017. 'The Eusebian Valorization of Violence and Constantine's Wars for God'. In *Constantine: Religious Faith and Imperial Policy*, edited by A. Edward Siecienski and Stockton University, 115–28. London: Routledge, Taylor & Francis Group.

DiCenso, James. 2011. *Kant, Religion, and Politics*. Cambridge: Cambridge University Press.

Dubuisson, Daniel. 2007. *The Western Construction of Religion: Myths, Knowledge, and Ideology*. Translated by William Sayers. Baltimore, MD: Johns Hopkins University Press.

Dupré, Louis. 1993. *Passage to Modernity: An Essay in the Hermeneutics of Nature and Culture*. New Haven, CT: Yale University Press.

Duquoc, Christian. 1985. 'Monotheism and Unitary Ideology'. In *Monotheism*, edited by Claude Geffré, Jean-Pierre Jossua, and Marcus Lefébure, 59–66. Concilium 177. Edinburgh: T. & T. Clark.

Erastus, Thomas. 1682. *A Treatise of Excommunication*. London: L. Curtis.

Feil, Ernst. 1992. 'From the Classical Religio to the Modern Religion: Elements of a Transformation between 1550 and 1650'. In *Religion in History: The Word, the Idea, the Reality*, edited by Michel Despland and Gérard Vallée, 31–43. Waterloo, Ontario, CA: Canadian Corporation for Studies in Religion/ Corporation Canadienne des sciences religieuses by Wilfrid Laurier University Press.

Fitzgerald, Timothy. 2007a. *Discourse on Civility and Barbarity: A Critical History of Religion and Related Categories*. New York: Oxford University Press.

——— ed. 2007b. *Religion and the Secular: Historical and Colonial Formations*. London: Equinox Pub.

Flood, Gavin Dennis. 2020. *Hindu Monotheism*. Cambridge: Cambridge University Press. https://doi.org/10.1017/9781108584289.

Gandhi, Mohandas. 2009. *M. K. Gandhi: Hind Swaraj and Other Writings*. Edited by Anthony J. Parel. 2nd ed. Cambridge: Cambridge University Press. http://ebooks.cambridge.org/ref/id/CBO9780511807268.

Geffré, Claude, Jean-Pierre Jossua, and Marcus Lefébure, eds. 1985. *Monotheism*. Concilium 177. Edinburgh: T. & T. Clark.

Girard, René, Jean-Michel Oughourlian, and Guy Lefort. 2016. *Things Hidden since the Foundation of the World*. Translated by Stephen Bann and Michael Leigh Metteer. London: Bloomsbury Academic.

Gray, Phillip W. 2007. 'Political Theology and the Theology of Politics: Carl Schmitt and Medieval Christian Political Thought'. *Humanitas* 20 (1–2): 175–200.

Grotius, Hugo, and G. H. M. Posthumus Meyjes. 1988. *Meletius, Sive, De Iis Quae Inter Christianos Conveniunt Epistola*. Studies in the History of Christian Thought, vol. 40. Leiden: Brill.

Grotius, Hugo, and Richard Tuck. 2005. *The Rights of War and Peace*. Indianapolis, IN: Liberty Fund.

Grzymała-Busse, Anna Maria. 2023. *Sacred Foundations: The Religious and Medieval Roots of the European State*. Princeton: Princeton University Press.

Habermas, Jürgen. 2019. *Auch eine Geschichte der Philosophie: Die okzidentale Konstellation von Glauben und Wissen*. 2 vols. Berlin: Suhrkamp.

Haring, James W. 2017. '"The Lord Your God Is God of Gods and Lord of Lords": Is Monotheism a Political Problem in the Hebrew Bible?' *Political Theology* 18 (6): 512–27. https://doi.org/10.1080/1462317X.2016.1263028.

Harrison, Peter. 1990. *'Religion' and the Religions in the English Enlightenment*. Cambridge: Cambridge University Press. https://doi.org/10.1017/CBO9780511627972.

——— 2017. *The Territories of Science and Religion*. Chicago: University of Chicago Press.

Hart, David Bentley. 2009. *Atheist Delusions: The Christian Revolution and Its Fashionable Enemies*. New Haven, CT: Yale University Press.

——— 2013. *The Experience of God: Being, Consciousness, Bliss*. New Haven, CT: Yale University Press.

Harvey, Peter. 2019. *Buddhism and Monotheism*. Cambridge: Cambridge University Press. https://doi.org/10.1017/9781108758390.

Harvey, Ramon. 2021. *Transcendent God, Rational World: A Māturīdī Theology*. Edinburgh: Edinburgh University Press.

Haw, Christopher A. 2021. *Monotheism, Intolerance, and the Path to Pluralistic Politics*. Cambridge: Cambridge University Press.

Haynes, Jeffrey, ed. 2021. *A Quarter Century of the 'Clash of Civilizations'.* London: Routledge. https://doi.org/10.4324/9781003161240.

Hedley, Douglas. 2016. *The Iconic Imagination.* New York: Bloomsbury Academic.

Hooker, Richard. 1989. *Of the Laws of Ecclesiastical Polity.* Cambridge: Cambridge University Press.

Hovorun, Archimandrite Cyril. 2022. 'Russian Church and Ukrainian War'. *The Expository Times* 134 (1): 1–10. https://doi.org/10.1177/0014524622 1119120.

Hume, David, John Charles Addison Gaskin, David Hume, and David Hume. 2008. *Principle Writings on Religion, Including Dialogues Concerning Natural Religion and the Natural History of Religion.* Oxford World's Classics. Oxford: Oxford University Press.

Huntington, Samuel P. 1996. *The Clash of Civilizations and the Remaking of World Order.* New York: Simon & Schuster.

Hurd, Elizabeth Shakman. 2008. *The Politics of Secularism in International Relations.* Princeton: Princeton University Press.

Hurtado, Larry W. 2005. *Lord Jesus Christ: Devotion to Jesus in Earliest Christianity.* Grand Rapids, MI: Eerdmans.

Ibrahim, Celene. 2022. *Islam and Monotheism.* New York: Cambridge University Press.

John, Ottmar. 1996. 'Zur Politik Der Theodizze'. In *Demokratiefähigkeit*, edited by Jürgen Manemann, 1:53–81. Jahrbuch Politisce Theologie.

Juergensmeyer, Mark. 2017. *Terror in the Mind of God: The Global Rise of Religious Violence.* Oakland, CA: University of California Press.

Juergensmeyer, Mark, Margo Kitts, and Michael K. Jerryson, eds. 2013. *The Oxford Handbook of Religion and Violence.* New York: Oxford University Press.

Kant, Immanuel. 1996. 'Religion within the Boundaries of Mere Reason'. In *Religion and Rational Theology*, edited by Allen W. Wood, translated by George Di Giovanni, 39–216. Cambridge: Cambridge University Press.

——— 1998. *Critique of Pure Reason.* Translated by Paul Guyer and Allen W. Wood. Cambridge: Cambridge University Press.

Kantorowicz, Ernst H. 2016. *The King's Two Bodies: A Study in Medieval Political Theology.* Princeton: Princeton University Press.

Kilby, Karen. 2000. 'Perichoresis and Projection: Problems with Social Doctrines of the Trinity'. *New Blackfriars* 81 (956): 432–45.

——— 2010. 'Is an Apophatic Trinitarianism Possible?' *International Journal of Systematic Theology* 12 (1): 65–77. https://doi.org/10.1111/j.1468-2400.2009 .00494.x.

2020. 'The Trinity and Politics: An Apophatic Approach'. In *God, Evil and the Limits of Theology*, 45–60. New York: T&T Clark.

2021. 'Reply to Critics'. *Political Theology* 22 (5): 423–32. https://doi.org/ 10.1080/1462317X.2021.1955577.

King, Richard. 1999. *Orientalism and Religion: Postcolonial Theory, India and 'the Mystic East'*. London: Routledge.

Kippenberg, Hans G. 2020. 'Sacred Prefigurations of Violence: Religious Communities in Situations of Conflict'. In *Religious Violence in the Ancient World: From Classical Athens to Late Antiquity*, edited by Jitse H. F. Dijkstra and Christian Rudolf Raschle, 17–45. Cambridge: Cambridge University Press.

Koselleck, Reinhart. 2018. *Kritik und Krise: eine Studie zur Pathogenese der bürgerlichen Welt*. Frankfurt am Main: Suhrkamp.

Laclau, Ernesto, and Chantal Mouffe. 2001. *Hegemony and Socialist Strategy: Towards a Radical Democratic Politics*. 2nd ed. London: Verso.

Lang, Bernhard. 1988. 'Monotheismus'. In *Handbuch religionswissenschaftlicher Grundbegriffe*, edited by Hubert Cancik, Burkhard Gladigow, and Matthias Laubscher, 4:148–65. Stuttgart: Verlag W. Kohlhammer.

Lefort, Claude. 2006. 'The Permanence of the Theologico-Political?' In *Political Theologies: Public Religions in a Post-Secular World*, edited by Hent de Vries and Lawrence Eugene Sullivan, 148–87. New York: Fordham University Press.

Lombard, David. 1747. *A Succinct History of Ancient and Modern Persecutions*. London: S Birt.

Luther, Martin. 1966. 'To the Christian Nobility of the German Nation Concerning the Reform of the Christian Estate, 1520'. In *The Christian in Society*, edited by James Atkinson, 44:115–219. Luther's Works. Philadelphia: Fortress Press.

Mahmood, Saba. 2016. *Religious Difference in a Secular Age: A Minority Report*. Princeton: Princeton University Press.

Maimonides, Moses. 1956. *The Guide for the Perplexed*. Edited by Michael Friedländer. New York: Dover.

Manemann, Jürgen. 2002. *Carl Schmitt und die politische theologie: Politischer anti-monotheismus*. Münsterische Beiträge zur Theologie, Bd. 61. Münster: Aschendorff.

Markschies, Christoph. 2010. 'The Price of Monotheism: Some New Observations on a Current Debate about Late Antiquity'. In *One God*, edited by Stephen Mitchell and Peter Van Nuffelen, 1st ed., 100–11. Cambridge: Cambridge University Press. https://doi.org/10.1017/CBO97805117 30115.007.

Markus, Robert Austin. 1988. *Saeculum: History and Society in the Theology of St. Augustine*. Cambridge: Cambridge University Press.

Marquard, Odo. 1989. 'In Praise of Polytheism (On Monomythical and Polymythical Thinking)'. In *Farewell to Matters of Principle: Philosophical Studies*, 87–110. Odéon. New York: Oxford University Press.

Marx, Karl. 1994. 'On the Jewish Question'. In *Marx: Early Political Writings*, edited by Joseph J. O'Malley, 28–56. Cambridge: Cambridge University Press.

Massa, Francesco. 2017. 'Nommer et classer les religions aux iie-ive siècles : la taxinomie « paganisme, judaïsme, christianisme'. *Revue de l'histoire des religions*, 234: 689–715. https://doi.org/10.4000/rhr.8829.

Masuzawa, Tomoko. 2005. *The Invention of World Religions, or, How European Universalism Was Preserved in the Language of Pluralism*. Chicago, IL: University of Chicago Press.

McCabe, Herbert. 2005. *God Matters*. Continuum Icons. London: Continuum.

McCarraher, Eugene. 2019. *The Enchantments of Mammon: How Capitalism Became the Religion of Modernity*. Cambridge, MA: The Belknap Press of Harvard University Press.

McCutcheon, Russell. 2007. '"They Licked the Platter Clean": On the Co-Dependency of the Religious and The Secular'. *Method & Theory in the Study of Religion* 19 (3): 173–99. https://doi.org/10.1163/157006807X240109.

McFarland, Ian A. 2019. *The Word Made Flesh: A Theology of the Incarnation*. Louisville, KY: Westminster John Knox Press.

McGrath, James F. 2009. *The Only True God: Early Christian Monotheism in Its Jewish Context*. Urbana, OH: University of Illinois Press.

Mehring, Reinhard. 2014. *Carl Schmitt: A Biography*. Translated by Daniel Steuer. Cambridge: Polity.

Milbank, John. 1995. 'Stories of Sacrifice: From Wellhausen to Girard'. *Theory, Culture & Society* 12 (4): 15–46.

2006. *Theology and Social Theory: Beyond Secular Reason*. Oxford: Blackwell.

Mills, Kenneth. 1997. *Idolatry and Its Enemies: Colonial Andean Religion and Extirpation, 1640–1750*. Princeton: Princeton University Press.

Møller, Jørgen, and Jonathan Stavnskær Doucette. 2022. *The Catholic Church and European State Formation, AD 1000–1500*. Oxford: Oxford University Press.

Moltmann, Jürgen. 1986. 'Christian Theology and Political Religion'. In *Civil Religion and Political Theology*, edited by Leroy S. Rouner, 41–58. 8. Notre Dame, IN: University of Notre Dame Press.

1993. *The Trinity and the Kingdom: The Doctrine of God*. Minneapolis, MN: Fortress Press.

More, Henry. 1660. *An Explanation of the Grand Mystery of Godliness*. London: Printed by J. Flesher, for W. Morden bookseller in Cambridge.

Mrówczyński-Van Allen, Artur. 2017. 'Beyond Political Theology and Its Liquidation: From Theopolitical Monotheism to Trinitarianism'. *Modern Theology* 33 (4): 570–93. https://doi.org/10.1111/moth.12356.

Nancy, Jean-Luc. 2003. 'The War of Monotheism 1'. *Postcolonial Studies* 6 (1): 51–3. https://doi.org/10.1080/13688790308116.

Naphy, William G. 2003. *Calvin and the Consolidation of the Genevan Reformation: With a New Preface*. Louisville, KY: Westminster John Knox Press.

Nelson, Eric. 2010. *The Hebrew Republic: Jewish Sources and the Transformation of European Political Thought*. Cambridge, MA: Harvard University Press.

Nicholls, David. 1989. *Deity and Domination*. London: Routledge.

Nongbri, Brent. 2013. *Before Religion: A History of a Modern Concept*. New Haven, CT: Yale University Press.

Oakley, Francis. 2006. *Kingship: The Politics of Enchantment*. Malden, MA: Blackwell Pub.

O'Donovan, Oliver. 2005. *The Desire of the Nations: Rediscovering the Roots of Political Theology*. Cambridge: Cambridge University Press.

Pépin, Jean. 1956. 'La « théologie Tripartite » de Varron. Essai de Reconstitution et Recherche Des Sources'. *Revue Des Études Augustiniennes* 3–4: 265–94.

Peterson, Erik. 2011. 'Monotheism as a Political Problem: A Contribution to the History of Political Theology in the Roman Empire'. In *Theological Tractates*, edited by Michael J. Hollerich, 68–105. Stanford: Stanford University Press.

Pitkin, Hanna Fenichel. 1967. *The Concept of Representation*. Berkeley, CA: University of California Press.

Pocock, J. G. A. 1997. 'Enthusiasm: The Antiself of Enlightenment'. *Huntington Library Quarterly* 60 (1/2): 7–28. https://doi.org/10.2307/3817830.

Prevot, Andrew. 2021. 'Karen Kilby on the Politics of Not Knowing'. *Political Theology* 22 (5): 373–78. https://doi.org/10.1080/1462317X.2021.1955571.

Pufendorf, Samuel. 2002. *Of the Nature and Qualification of Religion in Reference to Civil Society*. Edited by Simone Zurbuchen. Translated by Jodocus Crull. Indianapolis, IN: Liberty Fund.

Reeh, Niels. 2020. 'Inter-Religious Conflict, Translation, and the Usage of the Early Modern Notion of "Religion" from the Fall of Constantinople to the Westphalian Peace Treaty in 1648'. *Journal of Religion in Europe* 13 (1–2): 96–120. https://doi.org/10.1163/18748929-13010003.

Rose, Gillian. 1992. *The Broken Middle: Out of Our Ancient Society*. Oxford: Wiley-Blackwell.

———. 1996. *Mourning Becomes the Law: Philosophy and Representation*. Cambridge, UK: Cambridge University Press.

———. 2009. *Hegel Contra Sociology*. London: Verso.

Rousseau. 2012. 'Émile Ou de L'Éducation'. In *Oeuvres Complétes*, 8:668–1023. Éditions Slatkine: Geneve.

Ruggieri, Giuseppe. 1985. 'God and Power: A Political Function of Monotheism?' In *Monotheism*, edited by Claude Geffré, Jean-Pierre Jossua, and Marcus Lefébure, 16–27. Concilium 177. Edinburgh: T. & T. Clark.

Schaper, Joachim. 2019. *Media and Monotheism: Presence, Representation, and Abstraction in Ancient Judah*. Orientalische Religionen in Der Antike 33. Tübingen: Mohr Siebeck.

Schieder, Rolf. 2008. *Sind Religionen gefährlich?* Berlin: Berlin University Press.

———, ed. 2014. *Die Gewalt des einen Gottes: die Monotheismus-debatte zwischen Jan Assmann, Micha Brumlik, Rolf Schieder, Peter Sloterdijk und anderen*. Erste Auflage. Berlin: Berlin University Press.

Schindler, Alfred, ed. 1978. *Monotheismus als politisches Problem? Erik Peterson u.d. Kritik d. polit. Theologie*. Studien zur evangelischen Ethik, Bd. 14. Gütersloh: Gütersloher Verlagshaus Mohn.

Schmitt, Carl. 2005. *Political Theology: Four Chapters on the Concept of Sovereignty*. Translated by George Schwab. Chicago: University of Chicago Press.

———. 2007. *The Concept of the Political*. Translated by George Schwab. Chicago: University of Chicago Press.

———. 2008. *Political Theology II: The Myth of the Closure of Any Political Theology*. Translated by Michael Hoelzl and Graham Ward. Cambridge: Polity.

Schneider, Laurel C. 2008. *Beyond Monotheism: A Theology of Multiplicity*. London: Routledge.

Schwartz, Regina M. 1997. *The Curse of Cain: The Violent Legacy of Monotheism*. Chicago: University of Chicago Press.

Scott, James C. 2020. *Seeing like a State: How Certain Schemes to Improve the Human Condition Have Failed*. New Haven: Yale University Press.

Silverstein, Adam J., Guy G. Stroumsa, and Mark Silk. 2015. 'The Abrahamic Religions as a Modern Concept'. In *The Oxford Handbook of the Abrahamic Religions*, edited by Adam J. Silverstein and Guy G. Stroumsa, 71–87.

Oxford: Oxford University Press. https://doi.org/10.1093/oxfordhb/9780199697762.013.27.

Skinner, Quentin. 2009. 'A Genealogy of the Modern State'. *British Academy* 162: 325–70.

Sloterdijk, Peter. 2009. *God's Zeal: The Battle of the Three Monotheisms*. Cambridge: Polity.

Smith, Johnatan Z. 1998. 'Religion, Religions, Religious'. In *Critical Terms for Religious Studies*, edited by Mark C. Taylor. Chicago: The University of Chicago Press.

Smith, Mark S. 2003. *The Origins of Biblical Monotheism: Israel's Polytheistic Background and the Ugaritic Texts*. Oxford: Oxford University Press.

2010. *God in Translation: Deities in Cross-Cultural Discourse in the Biblical World*. Grand Rapids, MI: W.B. Eerdmans.

Soskice, Janet. 2017. 'Why Creatio Ex Nihilo for Theology Today?' In *Creation Ex Nihilo: Origins, Development, Contemporary Challenges*, edited by Gary A. Anderson, 37–54. Notre Dame: University of Notre Dame Press.

Stark, Rodney. 2003. *One True God: Historical Consequences of Monotheism*. Princeton: Princeton University Press.

Steinmetz-Jenkins, Daniel. 2011. 'Jan Assmann and the Theologization of the Political'. *Political Theology* 12 (4): 511–30. https://doi.org/10.1558/poth.v12i4.511.

Stiegler, Stefan, and Uwe Swarat, eds. 2006. *Der Monotheismus als theologisches und politisches Problem*. Leipzig: Evangelische Verlagsanstalt.

Stoll, Abraham Dylan. 2009. *Milton and Monotheism*. Pittsburgh, PA: Duquesne University Press.

Stroumsa, Guy G. 2010. *A New Science: The Discovery of Religion in the Age of Reason*. Cambridge, MA: Harvard University Press.

2021. *The Idea of Semitic Monotheism: The Rise and Fall of a Scholarly Myth*. Oxford: Oxford University Press. https://doi.org/10.1093/oso/9780192898685.001.0001.

Sundermeier, Theo. 1997. 'Religion, Religions'. In *Dictionary of Mission: Theology, History, Perspectives*, edited by Karl Müller, Theo Sundermeier, Stephen B. Bevans, and Richard H. Bliese, 387–97. Maryknoll, NY: Orbis books.

Taylor, Charles. 2007. *A Secular Age*. Cambridge, MA: Belknap Press of Harvard University Press.

Vries, Hent de. 1999. *Philosophy and the Turn to Religion*. Baltimore, MD: Johns Hopkins University Press.

Ward, Graham. 2005. *Christ and Culture*. Malden, MA: Blackwell Pub.

West, Martin Litchfield. 1999. 'Towards Monotheism'. In *Pagan Monotheism in Late Antiquity*, edited by Polymnia Athanassiadi and Michael Frede, 21–40. Oxford: Clarendon Press; Oxford University Press.

Westerlund, David. 1985. *African Religion in African Scholarship: A Preliminary Study of the Religious and Political Background*. Stockholm: Almqvist & Wiksell International.

———. 2006. *African Indigenous Religions and Disease Causation: From Spiritual Beings to Living Humans*. Leiden: Brill. https://doi.org/10.1163/9789047407690.

Williams, Raymond. 2014. *Keywords: A Vocabulary of Culture and Society*. Oxford: Oxford University Press.

Williams, Rowan. 1991. 'Theological Integrity'. *New Blackfriars* 72 (847): 140–51. https://doi.org/10.1111/j.1741-2005.1991.tb07155.x.

———. 2021. 'A True Otherness'. *Political Theology* 22 (5): 393–97. https://doi.org/10.1080/1462317X.2021.1955574.

———. 2023. 'Negative Theology: Some Misunderstandings'. *Modern Theology*, March, moth.12852. https://doi.org/10.1111/moth.12852.

Winnerman, Jonathan. 2021. 'Egyptology and Political Theology: An Examination of the Ethics of Scholarship'. *Journal of Near Eastern Studies* 80 (1): 167–93. https://doi.org/10.1086/713392.

Winter, Tim, and Nader El-Bizri, eds. 2008. 'God: Essence and Attributes'. In *The Cambridge Companion to Classical Islamic Theology*. Cambridge: Cambridge University Press. https://doi.org/10.1017/CCOL9780521780582.

Cambridge Elements ⹀

Religion and Monotheism

Paul K. Moser

Loyola University Chicago

Paul K. Moser is Professor of Philosophy at Loyola University Chicago. He is the author of *God in Moral Experience; Paul's Gospel of Divine Self-Sacrifice; The Divine Goodness of Jesus; Divine Guidance; Understanding Religious Experience; The God Relationship; The Elusive God* (winner of national book award from the Jesuit Honor Society); *The Evidence for God; The Severity of God; Knowledge and Evidence* (all Cambridge University Press); and *Philosophy after Objectivity* (Oxford University Press); coauthor of *Theory of Knowledge* (Oxford University Press); editor of *Jesus and Philosophy* (Cambridge University Press) and *The Oxford Handbook of Epistemology* (Oxford University Press); and coeditor of *The Wisdom of the Christian Faith* (Cambridge University Press). He is the coeditor with Chad Meister of the book series *Cambridge Studies in Religion, Philosophy, and Society*.

Chad Meister

Affiliate Scholar, Ansari Institute for Global Engagement with Religion, University of Notre Dame

Chad Meister is Affiliate Scholar at the Ansari Institute for Global Engagement with Religion at the University of Notre Dame. His authored and co-authored books include *Evil: A Guide for the Perplexed* (Bloomsbury Academic, 2nd edition); *Introducing Philosophy of Religion* (Routledge); *Introducing Christian Thought* (Routledge, 2nd edition); and *Contemporary Philosophical Theology* (Routledge). He has edited or co-edited the following: *The Oxford Handbook of Religious Diversity* (Oxford University Press); *Debating Christian Theism* (Oxford University Press); with Paul Moser, *The Cambridge Companion to the Problem of Evil* (Cambridge University Press); and with Charles Taliaferro, *The History of Evil* (Routledge, in six volumes). He is the co-editor with Paul Moser of the book series *Cambridge Studies in Religion, Philosophy, and Society*.

About the Series

This Cambridge Element series publishes original concise volumes on monotheism and its significance. Monotheism has occupied inquirers since the time of the Biblical patriarch, and it continues to attract interdisciplinary academic work today. Engaging, current, and concise, the Elements benefit teachers, researched, and advanced students in religious studies, Biblical studies, theology, philosophy of religion, and related fields.

Cambridge Elements ≡

Religion and Monotheism

Elements in the Series

*Monotheism and Narrative Development of the Divine Character
in the Hebrew Bible*
Mark McEntire

God and Being
Nathan Lyons

Monotheism and Divine Aggression
Collin Cornell

Jewish Monotheism and Slavery
Catherine Hezser

Open Theism
Alan R. Rhoda

African Philosophy of Religion and Western Monotheism
Kirk Lougheed, Motsamai Molefe and Thaddeus Metz

Monotheism and Pluralism
Rachel S. Mikva

The Abrahamic Vernacular
Rebecca Scharbach Wollenberg

Monotheism and Fundamentalism: Prevalence, Potential, and Resilience
Rik Peels

Emotions and Monotheism
John Corrigan

Monotheism and Peacebuilding
John D Brewer

The Politics of Monotheism
Ragnar M. Bergem

A full series listing is available at: www.cambridge.org/er&m

Printed in the United States
by Baker & Taylor Publisher Services